Cooking with a Harvard Accent

Cooking with a Harvard Accent

A Collection of International Recipes from the Harvard Community

Melanie Marcus

PUBLISHED IN ASSOCIATION WITH HARVARD MAGAZINE

Houghton Mifflin Company Boston   1979

Library of Congress Cataloging in Publication Data
Marcus, Melanie.
Cooking with a Harvard accent.
Includes index.
1. Cookery, International.   I. Title.
TX725.A1M345   641.59   79–20794
ISBN 0–395–27783–3

Printed in the United States of America

V 10 9 8 7 6 5 4 3 2 1

To my family

Acknowledgments

SOME PEOPLE would rather give out the combination to their safe than an old family recipe for gumbo or pastry. Fortunately, I met many good cooks around Harvard who were generous with their culinary heritage. These people taught me a great deal about cooking and about the flavors of their ethnic past. I thank them all for their hospitality, which has enriched my life, and for their recipes, which have enabled me to share the wealth.

While the cookbook could not have been written without these willing chefs, others in the Harvard community contributed nearly as much. My colleagues at *Harvard Magazine,* who helped launch the project, were also invaluable throughout my research. Their assistance included sharing supplies and resources, as well as fine recipes for curried coleslaw and scalloped veal. The magazine also served as a convenient vehicle for bringing news of the cookbook to Harvard alumni, and the staff patiently sorted the many recipes that were sent to me there.

Countless others around Harvard offered further support. I am thankful to the librarians who guided my search for illustrations; the archivists who uncovered secrets from Harvard's gustatory past; the administrators who supplied news of their departments and programs; and the editors at Harvard's graduate schools who published my requests for recipes.

Of special assistance were the staff and associates of the Schlesinger Library (home of Radcliffe's fabulous cookbook collection), and I thank them for their friendly cooperation and interest in the book. I'm particularly grateful to culinary historian Barbara Wheaton, whose recipes appear in the first and last chapters of this collection. She is the one who advised me early on that "the cookbooks are really wonderful by themselves, but unless you actually make the recipes, they're like musical instruments that don't get played."

Several people helped me with specific research projects. I thank Diana Shaw — Radcliffe's heavyweight coxswain and the creator of the Tomato-Yogurt Crew Soup — who helped gather recipes from undergraduates. Victoria Morris, a good friend and an editor at Radcliffe, assisted with mailings to faculty and alumni. Hildreth Burnette Potts, an artist at Harvard's Semitic Museum, translated various gastronomic materials from French into English. And Connie Pollard, the marzipan expert of greater Boston, assisted in testing a number of recipes.

I am also indebted to Jennifer Torrey and Richard Sellmer, whose cheerful, careful assistance eased the tedious task of proofreading. And to Harvard mathematician Michael Harris, who takes a ribbing on page 203, for double checking my metric conversions.

Many thanks, also, to those photographers affiliated with Harvard who helped me in gathering illustrations for the book. Jim Harrison of *Harvard Magazine* provided the ones culled from Radcliffe's cookbooks, which comprise most of the art in these pages. John Lupo of the Harvard Biology Laboratories supplied the reproductions of the mushrooms on page 108 and of the shrimp on page 209.

Steven Borak photographed illustrations from books in the Countway Medical Library. And the reproductions of art from the Fogg Art Museum, along with most of the remaining illustrations in the book, were provided by Barry Donahue and Michael Nedzweski, both of the Fogg's photographic department.

I would also like to thank Helena Bentz, my editor at Houghton Mifflin, who escorted the manuscript through each phase of production.

In addition to those who offered formal assistance, my friends on the sidelines also coached me along. I thank Rick Roberts for his friendly scrutiny of my cooking and prose; Barbara Gale for her electric mixer, black bean soup, and suggestions; Jim Shapiro for his long-distance enthusiasm and recipes; and Bill Tennermann for his loving good humor and faith.

Finally, I thank my family — wonderful cooks all — who nurtured my culinary interests. My grandmother, from Russia, instructed me in the hearty basics. My father, a former mess officer, taught me cost-effective cooking. My mother, a retired caterer, showed me how to make food elegant.

I also appreciate the larger lesson they taught me — that good food tastes best when it's shared with good people.

Preface

THERE IS NO SUCH THING as a Harvard accent. Not today, anyway. Not anymore.

I learned that in 1973, when — fresh out of journalism school at the University of Iowa — I became assistant editor at *Harvard Today,* an alumni tabloid that soon merged with *Harvard Magazine.*

As a Harvard journalist, I quickly corrected my outdated notions about Harvard as the bastion of the New England aristocracy. Writing an article on college admissions, I discovered that only 30 percent of the undergraduates come from New England, and a full 60 percent receive financial aid. Later research revealed that as far back as the seventeenth century Harvard's classes included the sons of butchers and bakers as well as Puritan ministers, and even then their ranks welcomed such foreigners as Europeans, Bermudians, and Virginians like myself.

It didn't take long to realize that Harvard's strength is its very diversity and that the University is a gathering place for all sorts of interesting people. My reporting kept me in contact with a global contingent of students and professors engaged in provocative research at the College, graduate schools, libraries, and museums.

As I got to know the University better, I found that the rich diversity that characterizes Harvard's academic affiliates is also apparent among those who make up its vast support structure. Some eleven thousand people work at the University, including piano tuners and biochemists, fund-raisers and landscape architects, librarians and carpenters, journalists and cooks. They, too, make up an international pool of talent, reflecting the many ethnic populations of Boston and Cambridge.

After two years on the staff of Harvard's alumni publications, I began to write a column on Harvard collections. The project gave me the chance to explore Harvard's *nonhuman* resources: the world's largest ant collection at the Museum of Comparative Zoology; the collection of tropical flora at the Harvard Biology Laboratories; and on one occasion, the cookbooks at Radcliffe's Schlesinger Library.

The enthusiasm I brought to this last assignment was well rewarded. I enjoyed browsing among the three thousand cookbooks, scanning European and American recipes that dated back several centuries. The volumes were amusing as well as enlightening. They offered a rich slice of domestic and social history, revealing family customs, medical remedies, and rules governing women's lives. I was struck, too, by the beauty of several nineteenth-century cookbooks, which were full of engravings that flaunted the "new" art of lithography.

Although my interests in cooking and writing were both of long standing, this was the first time I had had the pleasure of combining them. The effects of the experience lingered, and, like a person who has just learned a new word and then hears it everywhere, I promptly began noticing food news around Harvard.

First, I found out about the E.R.A. bake sales, political fund-raisers sponsored by the *men* at the Harvard Law

School. Then I stumbled upon the Busch-Reisinger's exhibit of medieval cookie cutters. Eventually, I learned that Harvard evens owns a copy of the first printed cookbook, a fifteenth-century manual citing rules for play, sleep, and sex, as well as for food preparation.

These discoveries led to my curiosity about Harvard's own culinary history, and I was hardly surprised to find a book on the subject. *Diets and Riots* described the story as tumultuous from the start. Nathaniel Eaton and his wife, the first "masters" of Harvard College, set the tone back in 1639, when in addition to other more academic duties, they were responsible for providing the students' "commons." This meal plan included a morning and evening "bevers" of bread and beer (Harvard ran its own brewery until the early 1800s) and a hot midday meal featuring fish or meat.

As caterers the Eatons were miserable failures. The students complained about fish that was served with the guts still in place, pudding that lacked both butter and suet, and other crimes too unappetizing to report in a cookbook. In the end the students rioted and the Eatons fled to Virginia. But that was hardly the end of the trouble.

Rude behavior at mealtime marred much of Harvard's early history, and the dining halls soon became nurseries of rebellion. In 1761 students responded to an excess of mutton in their diet by a loud chorus of bleating during their meals. The Butter Rebellion of 1766 resulted in a student strike to protest the use of rancid, imported butter. (A line from a poem commemorating that event — "Behold, our butter stinketh" — has earned notoriety in Harvard lore and is still used occasionally to disparage Harvard fare.) Next, the Cabbage Rebellion erupted in 1807.'And the century was dotted with untitled outbursts featuring the throwing of tableware and unappreciated foods.

Remnants of these unseemly customs are evident at

Harvard even today, although the students have much less to complain about. In the private sanctum of the Harvard Lampoon Castle, food throwing and plate smashing still punctuate evening meals, although the activity is less a protest than it is a celebration.

In the University dining halls, food services have improved considerably. Today's undergraduates are offered a well-balanced and relatively imaginative menu, including a selection of fresh produce in season. They can compile their own salads, layer their own sundaes, and sample other opportunities provided by administrators who have read their Harvard history.

Food at Harvard? I began to envision a cookbook. I wanted it to represent the people who make up the University, along with a selection of their international recipes. I imagined spicy anecdotes from Harvard's ample past and handsome illustrations from its libraries and museums.

Admittedly, cooking is hardly the first thing that comes to mind when you think of Harvard, but what is even more unusual is the concept of tackling Harvard as a whole. Every Tub on Its Own Bottom is the motto that characterizes Harvard's decentralized bureaucracy. My vision of representing the entire community — faculty, students, employees, and alumni — posed an appealing challenge. Besides, writing a Harvard cookbook sounded like fun.

When I mentioned the idea to my colleagues at *Harvard Magazine,* the editors, particularly Kit Reed, shared my enthusiasm. He suggested that I take the proposal to the editors at Houghton Mifflin, who offered me the opportunity to pursue the project full time.

I started in the fall of 1978. First, I became a contributing editor for the magazine rather than an assistant editor. Then I got down to the business at hand. As Harvard's unofficial recipe collector I had to start dozens of grapevines.

I posted announcements in newsletters and on bulletin boards. I called the professors I had interviewed previously for articles — ichthyologists, musicologists, physicists, historians — this time seeking recipes, instead of news of their research. And I became a real bore at cocktail parties. Whenever I met someone with a Harvard connection, I quickly responded, "And do you cook?"

One of my methods — a mailing to Harvard faculty members — resulted in some interesting, but disappointing correspondence. Archibald Cox apologized that frying hamburger marked his greatest culinary achievement; John Kenneth Galbraith cited instant coffee as his personal forte; Robert Coles admitted that he often burns toast.

Frequently, those who declined — whatever their reasons — were nice enough to suggest other leads. Professor Edwin O. Wilson, an entomologist as well as sociobiologist, does not cook but kindly referred me to a British cookbook called *Why Not Eat Insects?* Other professors singled out their gourmet students, and students directed me to their epicurean professors, a nice surprise indicating a meeting of more than the minds at Harvard.

Fortunately, all of these efforts paid off in recipes — hundreds of them, in a variety of guises. Some were mailed to *Harvard Magazine*; some, delivered to my home. There were recipes jotted on envelopes, typed on computer printouts, penned in stylish calligraphy. In the end I had more than I could possibly use, and I faced the editorial task of selection.

Thankfully, some recipes were easily eliminated. All Same Grease, a description of New Guinea cannibalism submitted by a graduate student in anthropology, was promptly rejected. So was the one entitled Screaming Hawaiian Meatballs, which began with the command, "Take off all your clothes and roll around in fifteen pounds of hamburger meat." But most of the rejected recipes were less dramatic. I finally chose the ones that made the tastiest and most unusual dishes and represented the largest possible cross section of Harvard cooks.

Taste judgments were based upon "recipe testings," gala affairs held in my Cambridge apartment. For the first time, following a recipe became a matter of precision, not taste. My kitchen, heretofore outfitted for one independent cook, was converted into a laboratory. I bought the requisite scales and timers, and an indulgent assortment of gadgets. My spice rack was abandoned for a substantial spice table, which I stocked with aromatics from remote ethnic markets. Then, once or twice weekly, using my new resources, I stirred up a batch of recently acquired recipes. The laboratory blossomed into a garden of flavors and a rotation of friends plucked from the exotic buffets. Their opinions and mine determined the best from the rest.

After each recipe had been tested and approved, I rewrote it according to a standardized format. The revised version lists ingredients in the order of their use and provides both the standard measurements and convenient metric conversions. But despite these stylistic adaptations, each recipe still retains the idiosyncrasies of its contributor. While I occasionally adjusted a formula to serve four or six instead of thirty, I refrained from tampering with ingredients and techniques. Sometimes, however, I do suggest a garnish or topping. And frequently either the contributor or I myself suggest a quantitative range for an ingredient, so that instead of insisting that you use three tablespoons of curry powder, you are invited to add from one to five tablespoons.

The truth is that this cookbook, more than most you will find, provides ample opportunity to use your own judgment. This works better when making stews than it does when baking pastry, but even here personal preference should help shape the final product. The approach reflects my own style in the kitchen, as well as the views

(xvi)

of those featured in the book. Most of the contributors are not professional chefs. They are simply good cooks who have recipes they're proud of. They themselves vary ingredients and quantities according to mood or circumstance, and they encourage you likewise to take liberties with their recipes. Nothing, but *nothing*, is more individual than taste.

At the same time, I don't advocate hastily eliminating or making substitutions for uncommon ingredients. Locating fresh coriander and coconut oil in a Latin market or gourmet shop may take some effort, but the resulting Brazilian shrimp dish is certainly worth it. Tracking down exotic herbs and oils can expand your culinary horizons, and if you make the trip, I will not leave you stranded. When unfamiliar ingredients are called for in a recipe, I suggest other uses for these newly purchased items.

Here, then, is my sampling of the flavors of Harvard. I hope the collection introduces you to Harvard people with *all* their accents. Mostly, I invite you to try the recipes themselves. I've tried them all, and I never ate better!

Contents

Hors d'Oeuvres

[OVERLEAF] *Hors d'oeuvres in general use during the nineteenth century as pictured in* The Royal Cookery Book *by Jules Gouffé. This lavishly illustrated volume, published in London in 1883, is among the three thousand cookbooks housed at Radcliffe's Schlesinger Library.*

Dutch Ham and Endives Gratinées

Serves 4

A stained-glass mosaic advocating COURAGE, LOVE, AND PATIENCE overlooks the Whitman Room of the Schlesinger Library, where most of Radcliffe's three thousand cookbooks are kept. Barbara Wheaton, culinary historian, has abided by the message throughout fifteen years of research on European cuisine.

Wheaton, who teaches food history at the Harvard Extension School, plans to publish a culinary treatise spanning eight centuries of history. Part of her research has involved taking recipes from the delicate pages of Radcliffe's rare cookbooks to the burners and blenders of her modern kitchen. Among her favorite historic recipes is the one for Muscovite of Strawberries on page 275.

But Wheaton's culinary collection, like that at Radcliffe, is kept right up to date. This is her modern recipe for ham and endives baked in a cheese sauce that is seasoned with nutmeg. Wheaton discovered the dish during a visit to Holland and was charmed by its classic simplicity and taste.

> 4 endives or 12 stalks parboiled asparagus
> 1 teaspoon salt
> 2 tablespoons butter
> 2 tablespoons flour
> 1 cup milk (¼ L)
> 1 cup grated Gruyère (¼ L)
> 2 tablespoons grated Parmesan
>   salt and pepper to taste
>   nutmeg to taste
> 4 slices boiled ham

Clean the endives and place them in a large skillet. Cover them with water, add the teaspoon of salt, and bring to a boil. Lower the heat, cover, and simmer for 5 minutes. Drain the endives and let them cool. Gently squeeze out as much liquid as possible.

Melt the butter in a saucepan. Add the flour and stir over low heat 3–5 minutes. Pour on the milk and whisk until the sauce is thick and smooth. Remove the saucepan from the heat. Add half the Gruyère and all the Parmesan, stirring until they have melted completely. Season with salt, pepper, and nutmeg.

Lightly butter a shallow baking dish and coat the bottom with a little of the cheese sauce. Wrap each endive (or 3 stalks parboiled asparagus, drained) in a piece of ham so that the vegetable shows at each end. Arrange the bundles in the baking dish, with the seam side of the ham down.

Spoon on the rest of the sauce and sprinkle with the remaining Gruyère. Bake at 350°F (180°C) for 20–30 minutes, until the sauce is bubbling and the top is golden brown. If necessary, place under the broiler for a few minutes.

This character is no magician, he's a purveyor of cheese. The woodcut is featured in a fifteenth-century health guide called Hortus Sanitatis, or "Garden of Health." Published in Mainz in 1491, the book is found among the treasures of Harvard's Countway Medical Library.

Penerlee

(Armenian Cheese Turnovers)

Makes 2–3 dozen

A rmenians can determine where fellow Armenians come from by hearing their word for this delicate hors d'oeuvre made with phyllo dough. Those whose roots are in Erevan and thereabouts call it penerlee. Luise Vosgerchian, the Walter W. Naumburg Professor of Music, has her familial roots in this geographic region.

Vosgerchian, who has taught piano theory at Harvard for decades, is among a small but growing number of tenured women at the University. She enjoys a great advantage in balancing a career with family life: her mother, who hails from a town outside Erevan, lives and helps cook at the Vosgerchian home. This is her mother's recipe for penerlee, a favorite of the Vosgerchian family's and of piano students who visit.

> 1 3-ounce package cream cheese, softened (85 g)
> 3 tablespoons small-curd cottage cheese
> 2 cups grated, extra-sharp cheddar cheese (½ L)
> 1 egg, lightly beaten
>   white pepper to taste
>   celery salt to taste
> ¼ cup chopped fresh parsley (½ dL)
> 1 teaspoon lemon juice
>
> 2 sticks butter, melted
> ¼ pound phyllo dough (15 dkg)*

* These tissue-thin pastry sheets can be found in the refrigerator cases of Armenian, Greek, and Middle Eastern grocery stores, and some gourmet shops. Keep the phyllo refrigerated until the filling has been prepared and you are ready to make the pastries.

To make the filling, combine the first group of ingredients and stir to blend thoroughly.

Sandwich the phyllo sheets between two moist towels. Carefully lift a single sheet and place it horizontally on a flat work surface. Using a pastry brush, brush the sheet lightly and carefully with a little of the melted butter. Cut the sheet into four or five vertical strips.

Place a teaspoon of filling at the bottom of a strip, leaving about a 1-inch margin on three sides. Fold the bottom left corner of the dough up until it is flush with the right side of the strip, forming a triangle. Press the right edge to seal it, so that no filling can escape. Continue folding the triangles and pressing the seams to the top of the strip. Moisten the top flap with water to make a secure seam.

Repeat this process, strip by strip and sheet by sheet, until you have used up all of the filling. Place the penerlee on lightly greased cookie sheets. Bake at 350°F (180°C) for 20–30 minutes until golden brown.

Oeufs à la Paté Vite Restaurant

(Poached Eggs in Veal Stock with Mushrooms, Bacon, and Croutons)

Serves 4

Running, cooking, and writing keep Jim Shapiro pretty busy. Shapiro (Class of 1968) runs from his West Side apartment to the Paté Vite restaurant in Brooklyn, where he works as a chef. This gustatory

"Le Menu" is drawn from the pages of the Dictionnaire de l'académie des gastronomes, *part of the Schlesinger Library's culinary collection.*

nook offers an unusual selection of French haute cuisine, including a house specialty of poached eggs, given here, and a Rock Cornish hen with herbed stuffing (page 152).

Traveling to and from work takes Shapiro two hours daily, and the cooking itself occupies nine. What's left of his time and energy he devotes to writing — a book on marathon running and a novel about Harvard.

    4 **eggs**
    2 **tablespoons butter**
    4 **mushrooms, sliced**
        salt and pepper to taste
    2 **tablespoons olive oil**
  ½ **cup dried white bread cubes (1 dL)**
    4 **bacon strips, fried crisp and crumbled**
1½ **cups veal stock or undiluted beef consommé (3½ dL)**
    2 **tablespoons chopped fresh parsley**

(8)

Poach the eggs and then gently slide them into a bowl of cool water. Melt the butter in a skillet. Add the mushrooms, salt, and pepper, and cook for several minutes until the mushrooms are just soft. Remove them with a slotted spoon and set them aside. Heat the olive oil in a skillet and cook the bread cubes until they turn brown. In a small bowl, combine the mushrooms, bread cubes (now croutons), and bacon bits.

Place the mixture in four fairly deep, small bowls (just larger than the circumference of the poached egg). Using a slotted spoon, slide a poached egg into each bowl. Bring the veal stock or beef consommé to a boil and then pour some carefully into each dish, down the side, avoiding pressure on the egg yolks. Garnish with chopped parsley.

"Love Story" Gefilte Fish

Makes 20–30

Gerry Weinstock is president of Basic Foods (a division of Mallinckrodt, Inc.), which supplies specialized baking ingredients to food manufacturers. He is also a leader in the Harvard community. A graduate of the College in 1939 and the Law School in 1942, Weinstock is a former director of the Associated Harvard Alumni and helped organize Harvard's campaign to create the Center for Jewish Studies.

But the appellation that most befits Weinstock is that of storyteller. On the phone, in his business letters, while waiting for the elevator, Weinstock has a tale to fit every occasion, including how he acquired his recipe for gefilte fish. It seems that Gerry and his wife, Margaret (Class of

(9)

1945), were married by Rabbi Samuel Segal, whose son Erich (Class of 1958) wrote *Love Story*, a Harvard romance. Erich's mother, Cynthia, gave the Weinstocks this recipe. She also gave a version of the formula to Craig Claiborne, the *New York Times* food editor, who included it in a cookbook of favorite recipes from his column.

THE STOCK

    6 cups water (1½ L)
    2 onions, quartered
    2 carrots, sliced
    1 clove garlic
      heads, bones, and skin from pike and white fish
      salt and pepper to taste

THE FISH BALLS

    4–5 pounds pike and white fish fillets (2–2½ kg)
    3 large onions
    3 eggs, lightly beaten
      salt and pepper to taste

Combine the ingredients for the stock in a large pot, and slowly bring this to a boil. Meanwhile, grind the fish fillets and the onions in a food processor or by passing them through a food mill. Add the eggs, salt, and pepper, and stir to mix thoroughly. Form the mixture into balls or oval patties.

Strain the fish stock and return it to the stove. When the stock is boiling, gently drop the fish balls into it. Cover the pot, reduce the heat, and simmer for 1 hour. Remove the fish balls with a slotted spoon and let them cool.

Strain the stock again and save it for use as a base for soup (see Seafood Soup Anisette, page 41, and the Vietnamese Fish-Pineapple Chowder on page 31) or refrigerate the stock until it jells. Then chop and arrange it around the gefilte fish. This hors d'oeuvre is also served on lettuce or watercress with horseradish on the side and a slice of boiled carrot on top.

Skoombria

(Estonian Fish Hors d'Oeuvre)

Makes about 5 cups

C ooking and reading are common hobbies but few people combine them the way Joyce Toomre does. She reads literature — from Dickens to Gogol — with an eye for a tasty meal, as well as a well-turned phrase. Then she sets out to recreate the dishes. Toomre is a research associate in literature at Harvard's Russian Research Center. While reading the second part of Gogol's *Dead Souls,* she paid close attention to the fisherman Petux. From him she learned Russian recipes for carp, crayfish, and smelts.

Another unusual fish dish is her Estonian skoombria (Rússian for "mackerel"), which she prepares using New England cod and other white fish. Toomre cooks the fish with grated carrots, tomato paste, and seasonings. When completed, this fish paté is orange-red and delicious.

1 pound cod or other white fish, cut into large chunks
   (46 dkg)
¼ cup flour (½ dL)
   salt and pepper
½ cup vegetable oil (1 dL)
3 onions, finely chopped
4 carrots, grated
4 whole allspice
1 teaspoon paprika
1 12-ounce can tomato paste (34 dkg)
⅓ cup ketchup (¾ dL)
1 bay leaf
   salt and pepper to taste
1–2 tablespoons lemon juice
   lemon wedges and parsley for garnish

Dredge the cod in flour that has been seasoned with salt and pepper. Heat half the oil in a large pot or heavy casserole. Add the cod and cook over medium heat for 10–12 minutes, until barely done. Remove the cod with a slotted spoon and set it aside.

Add to the oil the onions, carrots, allspice, and paprika. Cook over low heat for 5 minutes. Return the cod to the pot. Add the tomato paste, ketchup, bay leaf, salt, and pepper. Stir and mash thoroughly. Cover and simmer for 45 minutes, stirring frequently. While simmering, add the remaining oil sparingly, as needed, to keep the mixture moist (like a tuna or crabmeat salad).

Cover the skoombria and refrigerate it for 24 hours. Before serving, add the lemon juice and stir to blend thoroughly. Mount the skoombria on a serving platter and garnish it with parsley and lemon wedges. Serve with thinly sliced black bread and butter.

Oliver dares to ask for more in this detail from a theater poster announcing the performance of Oliver Twist *at the Royal Surrey Theatre on November 19, 1838. The poster is among the theatrical ephemera found in the Harvard Theatre Collection, Pusey Library.*

Dickensian Horseradish Sauce for Oysters

Makes ⅓ cup

Joyce Toomre is particularly fond of the food consumed by Dickens's characters and is writing a cookbook based on her research. Taking culinary references from the stories themselves, she consults cookbooks at Radcliffe's Schlesinger Library to locate the recipes Dickens's contemporaries might have used.

Oysters were so popular in *The Posthumous Papers of the Pickwick Club* that Toomre wondered just how they were served. *The Professed Cook*, published in London in 1769, was among the resources on the Schlesinger shelves. The book suggested this recipe for horseradish sauce to go with oysters, and Toomre has adapted it for modern cooks. She serves it, along with such dishes as pigeon pie and seed cake, in Dickensian banquets for family and friends.

¼ cup chopped fresh parsley (½ dL)
3 scallions, minced
1 clove garlic, minced
½ teaspoon salt
¼ teaspoon pepper
1 teaspoon anchovy paste
½ teaspoon capers
1 tablespoon prepared horseradish
2 teaspoons vegetable oil
2 teaspoons vinegar
1 tablespoon heavy cream

Mix and mash together the parsley, scallions, garlic, salt, and pepper until they form a coarse paste. Add the remaining ingredients and stir to blend thoroughly. Serve as a sauce for fresh oysters or as a dip for boiled shrimp.

Cucumber Sandwiches for Asia Enthusiasts

Makes about 36

W hen John K. Fairbank and Wilma Cannon met as undergraduates, they didn't know they would make Harvard history. Together they traveled to China, were married in Peking, and stayed four more years.

Upon their return to Harvard in 1936, John Fairbank helped establish Asia courses, which he taught from that year until his retirement as Francis Lee Higginson Professor of History. Wilma Fairbank, an expert on East Asian art who has written two books on the subject, created her own Cambridge tradition — weekly open-house teas for Asia enthusiasts and other guests, featuring a menu of cucumber sandwiches and brownies.

The Fairbanks have extended this standard hospitality, nearly continuously, for forty years. You're welcome to sandwich the cucumbers yourself, or come join the party: 41 Winthrop Street, Thursday afternoons.

    1 loaf thinly sliced whole wheat bread *
    2 cucumbers, peeled and sliced
    1 8-ounce package cream cheese with chives (23 dkg)
    ⅓ cup mayonnaise (¾ dL)
      salt and pepper to taste

Spread the cream cheese with chives on half of the pieces of bread and the mayonnaise on the other half. Place

---

* The Fairbanks refrain from trimming the crusts because their student guests prefer to have more in each bite.

The Absolutely Abstemious Ass,
who resided in a barrel, and only
lived on Soda Water, and Pickled Cucumbers.

This pen and ink drawing by Edward Lear appeared in More
Nonsense, *published in London in 1872. It was reprinted as
a greeting card by the printing and graphic arts department
of Harvard's Houghton Library.*

four cucumber slices (one per quadrant) on each piece of bread with mayonnaise. Sprinkle with salt and pepper. Top with the complementary bread slice and cut into fourths.

Szechwan Pickle Relish

Serves 10

Peter Gourevitch appreciated the good selection of Chinese restaurants in Cambridge and Boston during his years as a student and then administrator at Harvard.

A doctoral recipient in 1970, Gourevitch was acting director of the Harvard Center for European Studies before accepting a position teaching political science at McGill University. When Gourevitch made the move from Cambridge to Montreal, he promptly scoured the city for a good Chinese restaurant. "'Montreal,'" he soon learned, "now favors other cuisines." Disappointed, Gourevitch enrolled in a cooking class offered by Dick Chen, a local expert. There he learned dozens of fine Chinese recipes, including this one for a simple yet exotic hors d'oeuvre.

    2 large cucumbers
    1 teaspoon salt
2–3 cups water (½–¾ L)
    6 tablespoons sugar
 4½ tablespoons white vinegar
1–2 teaspoons spicy bean sauce*
1–2 tablespoons sesame oil *

* Spicy bean sauce and sesame oil are sold in Chinese markets and gourmet shops. These days, the oil is also available in many supermarkets.

Slice the unpeeled cucumbers in half lengthwise and scoop out the seeds. Slice each piece in half lengthwise again and cut into 2-inch pieces. Place the salt and water in a bowl and stir. Add the cucumber pieces, cover the bowl, and let them soak for 3–5 hours.

Drain the cucumbers in a colander. Using the back of a spoon, gently squeeze out the excess water. Arrange the cucumber pieces in a serving dish. In a small bowl, combine and mix thoroughly the sugar, vinegar, and bean sauce. Pour this over the cucumbers. Cover and refrigerate them 1–2 hours. (The relish gets hotter as it matures.) Spoon on the sesame oil just before serving.

Uova Ripiene

(Italian Deviled Eggs)

Makes 16

For a snappy Italian version of deviled eggs, try the recipe Brian Ibsen discovered while living in northern Italy. A 1972 alumnus of Harvard's Graduate School of Education, Ibsen took a year off from teaching in Boston to work in an American school near Turin. While attending a benefit for victims of the Friuli earthquake, he purchased an Italian cookbook that included this colorful Piedmontese dish. The recipe makes delicate use of capers and anchovies. For those who generally find the flavor of these ingredients *too* potent, here is the dish that could change their mind.

8 hard-boiled eggs
1 3½-ounce can tuna, drained and flaked (100 g)
½ cup chopped black olives (1 dL)
¼ cup chopped fresh parsley (½ dL)
¼ cup capers (½ dL)
4 anchovies, drained, rinsed, and sliced
juice of 1 lemon
dash wine vinegar
2–4 tablespoons olive oil
sliced pimientos for garnish

Slice the hard-boiled eggs in half lengthwise. Scoop out the yolks and place them in a bowl. Reserve the whites. Add to the egg yolks the tuna, olives, parsley, capers, and anchovies. Mash and blend thoroughly. Add the lemon juice, vinegar, and enough olive oil to make a moist mixture. Combine thoroughly and then stuff the mixture into the egg whites. Garnish each egg with pimiento. Spread the excess stuffing on celery and crackers.

Mousse de Mer à la Sauce Verte

(Seafood Mousse with Green Sauce)

Serves 8

A professor of law and an antitrust expert, Phil Areeda is judicious about what he consumes. Formerly a counsel to Presidents Ford and Eisenhower, he now advises the Faculty Club's wine committee on "the least objectionable of the low-priced wines." And

Don Juan as played by Mr. Charles Kemble flourishes through the pen of artist J. Bailey. This nineteenth-century drawing comes from the collection of theatrical portraits found in the Harvard Theatre Collection, Pusey Library.

what does Areeda suggest to accompany Mousse de Mer?
"A white burgundy, preferably Chassagne-Montrachet."

THE MOUSSE

½ pound shrimp, shelled and deveined (23 dkg)
½ pound scallops (23 dkg)
4 egg whites
½ teaspoon salt
¼ teaspoon pepper
¼ teaspoon nutmeg
¼ teaspoon dill
½ pint heavy cream (¼ L)
3–4 cups boiling water (¾ to 1 L)
parsley sprigs for garnish

Butter a 1-quart (1-L) oval baking dish. Cut two ovals
of waxed paper to fit inside the dish and butter one side
of each. Place one sheet in the bottom of the dish, buttered side up.

Purée the shrimp (reserving several to cook for garnish) and the scallops in a food processor or blender or
by passing them through a food mill. Place the purée in
a large bowl. Add the egg whites, salt, pepper, nutmeg,
and dill. Beat until frothy. Add the cream and beat until
the mixture has a batterlike consistency. Pour the contents of the bowl into the prepared baking dish, and place
the remaining sheet of waxed paper on top, buttered side
down.

Pour the boiling water into a roasting pan until it is a
third full. Put the mousse in the middle and place the
roasting pan in the center of the oven. Bake at 375°F
(190°C) for 40 minutes or until a toothpick (slipped under the waxed paper) inserted into the center comes out
clean.

Let the mousse cool to room temperature. Cover and
refrigerate for at least 4 hours. Unmold the mousse onto

(21)

a serving platter. Cover any surface imperfections with whole, cooked shrimp and parsley. Slice, and serve with the Sauce Verte.

THE SAUCE

1	egg
1	tablespoon lemon juice
1	teaspoon salt
¼	teaspoon pepper
1	cup olive oil (¼ L)
1	teaspoon tarragon
1–2	teaspoons dill
6	scallions, minced
6–12	parsley sprigs, chopped
4–8	spinach leaves, chopped

Whirl the egg, lemon juice, salt, and pepper in a food processor or blender. Add ½ cup (1 dL) of the olive oil drop by drop, blending until the oil is absorbed. Blend in the remaining oil by teaspoonfuls. Add the remaining ingredients and blend thoroughly.

Expatriot Guacamole

Makes about 4 cups

Tony Kahn (Class of 1966) spent part of his childhood in Hollywood and moved to Cuernavaca in 1950. That was the year that his father, scriptwriter Gordon Kahn, fled to Mexico to avoid being subpoenaed by the House Un-American Activities Committee. The elder Kahn wrote forty scripts, including *All*

Quiet on the Western Front and *The Cowboy and the Señorita* (the first Roy Rogers–Dale Evans film).

In Cuernavaca, Tony adjusted to the flavors of Mexico with the help of Simona, the Kahn's cook. One family favorite was Simona's guacamole — a perfect combination of lemon, onion, and avocado. Now a Cambridge-based writer for film and television, Tony makes the guacamole himself. He continues to enjoy Simona's blend on corn chips, in sandwiches, and straight from the bowl.

   3 **ripe avocados**
   3 **tablespoons mayonnaise**
      juice of 2 lemons
   5 **cloves garlic, pressed**
¼ **teaspoon salt**
      pepper to taste
   1 **large onion, finely chopped**

Slice the avocados in half lengthwise and scoop the meat into a large bowl. Mash until smooth. Add the mayonnaise and blend. Add all but 2 tablespoons of the lemon juice to this mixture. Add the garlic, salt, and pepper. Press a little of the chopped onion in a garlic press and mix the onion juice into the mashed avocado. Add the pressed onion pulp, along with the rest of the chopped onion. Stir to mix thoroughly. Pour the remaining lemon juice over the top to delay discoloration. Cover the guacamole and refrigerate it for at least 3 hours. Before serving, stir to blend in the lemon juice.

Fried Day Lilies and
Squash Blossoms

I f you have a garden, or access to one, consider eating a few of the flowers. Day lilies, for example, which last only one day, can be made into wonderful, crispy hors d'oeuvres. This neighborly advice comes from Jane Watkins, who harvests her lilies on summer evenings at dusk.

Watkins is the director of Harvard Neighbors, a resource center for newcomers to the University. She supplies information on housing, day care, athletic facilities, and the like, and organizes such activities as University tours and parties. She also coordinates a series of classes in subjects like gardening and cooking.

A novelist as well as an official hostess for Harvard, Watkins notes that her culinary specialty is not limited to lilies. The technique she describes here works with squash blossoms, too. Be sure to pick the male squash flowers, Watkins advises. These are the ones that do not produce squash and do not have bulbous ovaries between them and the stalk.

> day lilies or male squash blossoms
> flour
> salt
> egg whites, lightly beaten
> vegetable oil for deep frying

Dip the day lilies or squash blossoms in flour that has been seasoned with salt. Then dip them in the egg whites, and once again in the flour. Heat the oil in a deep pot.

Fry the blossoms in the hot oil for 1–2 minutes, until golden brown. Drain them on paper towels. Serve the fried blossoms plain, sprinkled with salt, or with Chinese duck sauce.

This seventeenth-century engraving of the female squash blossom identifies the flower one should not pick for frying. (Note the bulbous ovary between the flower and the stalk, which produces the squash.) This illustration first appeared in a botanical capacity as part of Hortus Indicus Malabaricus, *by Van Rheede tot Draakestein. The book, published in Amsterdam in 1688, is found among the rare works at Harvard's Gray Herbarium Library.*

Potato Latkes

Makes 20–30

For absolute authenticity, these latkes should be served by a nervous six-year-old in pajamas," reports free-lance writer Laura Shapiro (Class of 1968). Obviously, Shapiro's interest in these Eastern European pancakes was sparked at an early age. Since then, her culinary interests have matured and expanded to include, among other things, the Indian appetizer that follows. Most recently she has directed her attention to the advent of scientific cooking.

While browsing through *Notable American Women* (an encyclopedia published by the Harvard University Press), Shapiro was intrigued by the entry on Fannie Farmer, the first purveyor of precise measurements in cooking and baking, and, of course, founder of Miss Farmer's School of Cookery. Shapiro's interest in her was heightened by a feminist tour through Cambridge's Mount Auburn Cemetery, where she saw Fannie Farmer's tomb. She is now writing a book about Fannie Farmer and her pioneering approach to scientific cookery.

    4 potatoes, peeled and diced
    2 eggs
    1 small onion, finely chopped
    ¼ cup flour (½ dL)
    1½ teaspoons salt
      pepper to taste
      vegetable shortening for frying

In a blender, combine the potatoes, eggs, and onion. Blend just until the liquid rises to the top. (Or grate the potatoes, finely chop the onions, and combine them with the beaten eggs.) Pour the mixture into a bowl. Stir in the flour, salt, and pepper.

Melt the shortening in a large skillet. Drop the potato mixture by spoonfuls into the skillet and fry over medium heat for several minutes on each side until golden brown and crisp. Drain the latkes on paper towels. Serve with a dollop of sour cream or applesauce.

If you wish to freeze the latkes so that you can always have some on hand, fry them but do not drain them. Place them on a cookie sheet and refrigerate them for 30 minutes before putting them in a plastic bag and freezing them. When you want to serve the latkes, place them on a cookie sheet and heat them in a 400°F (205°C) oven for 10–15 minutes. Drain on paper towels before serving.

Indian Spinach Pakoras

Makes 20–25

Laura Shapiro learned to make these deep-fried hors d'oeuvres from an American cellist who lived in Benares, India. His version, unlike many Indian recipes for pakoras, incorporates the chopped vegetables *into* the batter, rather than having them sealed inside a pastry shell. Pakoras can be made with eggplant, cauliflower, potato, or whatever is handy. In India, they are served with chutney.

(27)

1¼ cups graham or chickpea flour (3 dL) *
¾ teaspoon salt
¾ teaspoon ground cumin
   pepper to taste
½ cup cold water (1 dL)
1 cup coarsely chopped spinach (¼ L)
1 small onion, finely chopped
1½ cups vegetable oil (3½ dL)

In a bowl combine the flour, salt, cumin, and pepper. Add the water and stir to form a smooth batter. Add the chopped spinach and onion. If the mixture feels too dry to handle easily, add another 1–2 tablespoons water.

Heat the oil to 365°F (180°C) in a deep skillet. Drop the batter by teaspoonfuls into the skillet and fry over medium-high heat until golden brown all over. Drain the pakoras on paper towels and serve them with chutney. Try the Date-Raisin Chutney on page 247.

---

* Chickpea flour is sold in Indian and African specialty stores and some gourmet shops.

Soups

Cahn Chua

(Vietnamese Fish-Pineapple Chowder)

Serves 8–10

R andy Gillerman went to Vietnam in 1972 and settled in the Mekong Delta to conduct anthropolog-
ical research. She lived, surrounded by war, in the
village of My-Duc, a fishing community two kilometers
from the Cambodian border. Her prompt mastery of the
language convinced Gillerman's neighbors that she had
been Vietnamese in a previous existence.

Today Gillerman and her adopted Vietnamese son live
in Holden Green, Harvard's international housing complex
for graduate students. Now a doctoral candidate in psychology at Harvard, Gillerman uses psycho-linguistics to
study Vietnamese speech patterns. Her data come from
interviews with some of the two thousand Vietnamese
immigrants living in Greater Boston.

One of the women Gillerman interviewed, Mrs. Liem Truong, became a friend. She helped quantify the ingredients in this fondly remembered piquant chowder. Cahn chua ("sour soup"), like the Vietnamese language, has many regional variations. This one, typically southern, represents the province where Gillerman, her son, and Liem used to live.

½   cup peanut or other oil (1 dL)
4   cloves garlic, sliced
3   cups fresh pineapple chunks (¾ L)
2–4 tablespoons sugar
2   pounds shelled whole shrimp or white fish fillets cut
      into chunks (90 dkg)
3   cups fish stock (¾ L)
1½ teaspoons salt
½   cup fish sauce (1 dL)*
½–¾ cup lemon juice or vinegar (1–1¾ dL)
2–3 tomatoes, cut into chunks
2–3 celery stalks, trimmed of leaves and cut on the
      diagonal into 1½-inch pieces
1   small onion, thinly sliced
½   cup sliced scallion greens (1 dL)
1   small, hot red pepper with seeds, sliced
½   teaspoon ground cumin
1   teaspoon monosodium glutamate
1½ cups bean sprouts (3½ dL)

Heat the oil in a large pot. Add the garlic and cook over a medium-high heat until golden brown. Using a slotted spoon, remove the garlic slices and discard them. Add the

* Sold in Oriental (particularly Vietnamese) markets, fish sauce may bear the Vietnamese name *nuoc mam*, meaning "water of fish." The sauce adds a nice flavor to soups and stir-fried dishes. Also, to make a Vietnamese sauce for a seafood crepe, add a tablespoon or so to 3 tablespoons water, 1 tablespoon lemon juice, 1 teaspoon sugar, and 2 crushed cloves of garlic.

pineapple and sugar and stir-fry for 3–5 minutes. Remove the pineapple with a slotted spoon and set it aside. If using shrimp, add them to the flavored oil and stir-fry until nearly firm. Remove them with a slotted spoon and set them aside.

Add to the oil the fish stock, salt, fish sauce, and most of the lemon juice or vinegar. If using fish, add it now and simmer it in the liquid for 5 minutes. Add the tomatoes, celery, onion, scallion greens, hot pepper, cumin, and monosodium glutamate. Return the shrimp to the pot. Simmer for 3–5 minutes. Adjust the flavors, adding more fish sauce and lemon juice or vinegar to taste. Add the bean sprouts and stir once. Serve over boiled rice with hot red-pepper flakes to taste.

Veritasty Clam Chowder

Serves 10

Joe Purcell, head chef at Harvard's Faculty Club, begins making chowder every Friday at 6 A.M. In two hours he stirs up a full sixty gallons, and by 8 P.M. the caldron has been drained. Purcell's efforts feed a substantial crowd, but his scaled-down version is just right for chefs with fewer clients.

This soup is identified simply on the Faculty Club menu as "clam chowder." Here it is named for its full, honest flavor and for the *Veritas* on Harvard's seal.

     1 dozen quahogs or other clams
     1 tablespoon cream of tartar
    1½ quarts water (1½ L)
     1 bay leaf
     2 parsley sprigs
       pepper to taste
     4 tablespoons butter
     1 large onion, finely chopped
     ½ cup diced bacon or salt pork (1 dL)
     3 tablespoons flour
     2 large potatoes, peeled and diced
     3 cups milk (¾ L)
    1½ pints light cream (¾ L)
       hot-pepper sauce to taste
       salt to taste
     2 small French rolls, sliced into 10 rounds
       butter
     4 teaspoons dried parsley flakes
     4 teaspoons paprika

Soak the clams for 15 minutes in water to which cream of tartar has been added. Scrub the clams and rinse them with cold water several times. In a large pot, combine the water, bay leaf, parsley, and pepper. Bring this to a boil, add the clams, and cook them until the shells open, about 5 minutes. Remove the clams from the shells, rinse, and chop them. Skim the stock and let it simmer uncovered until it is reduced to about half its original volume.

Meanwhile, melt the butter in a large pot. Add the onions and bacon, and cook until the onions turn golden. Add the flour, mix thoroughly, and stir over low heat for 5 minutes. Add the chopped clams and whisk in 3 cups (¾ L) of the reduced stock. Add the potatoes and boil them until they are tender. Remove the pot from the heat and keep it covered while you heat the milk and cream in a saucepan. Add this to the large pot and cook the chowder over low heat for 10 minutes, stirring constantly.

Add the hot-pepper sauce and salt. Cover the pot while preparing the garnish.

Butter the bread rounds and toast them in the oven at 350°F (180°C) until golden brown. Holding a knife blade-down across the center of each round, sprinkle one side with parsley flakes and the other side with paprika. Serve the clam chowder in large bowls, and float one crouton on top of each serving.

Two-Faced Fish Chowder

Serves 8

As editor of publications for alumnae of Radcliffe, Aida Press is responsible for two periodicals — the *Radcliffe Quarterly* and the *Centennial News*, a news-feature tabloid.

Press is known for only one culinary specialty — fish chowder — but she feels that this is an underestimation of her talents in the kitchen. Her recipe can be based upon milk or tomatoes. Press likes to point out that she makes *both* versions well.

2 cups water (½ L)
2 small potatoes, peeled and thinly sliced
2 pounds haddock, cut into several pieces (90 dkg)
1 onion, finely chopped
2 bay leaves
4 cups milk at room temperature *or* a combination of tomato juice and stewed tomatoes and their liquid (1 L)
  salt to taste
2 tablespoons butter
  paprika for garnish

The cover of a cookbook by Annette Lucas published in Paris in the late 1800s and now housed at Radcliffe's Schlesinger Library.

Boil the water in a large pot. Add the sliced potatoes and simmer for 5 minutes. Add the haddock and simmer for another 10 minutes, stirring occasionally. (Once the haddock has simmered for a few minutes, it is easy to scrape off the skin with a spoon.) Add the onion and bay leaves. Then add the milk or the tomato combination. Simmer for another 10 minutes. Remove the chowder from the heat, taste it and then season with salt. Add the butter and stir until it melts. Remove the bay leaves. Sprinkle the milk version with paprika for color.

Aida Press serves the chowder with oyster crackers or water biscuits. Her soup, like most, tastes even better the second day.

Two Tabasco Recipes for Oyster Bisque

Walter McIlhenney's family owns the Tabasco sauce business as well as Avery Island, Louisiana, where the hot peppers are grown. Since the 1860s, when Edmund McIlhenny invented the sauce, his family's recipes have been seasoned with its fiery flavor. Tasty examples are these oyster bisque recipes — the original family formula of 1868 and the version revised a hundred years later.

The McIlhennys are associated with Harvard's Peabody Museum of Archaeology and Ethnology. In 1934 they presented the museum with a collection of baskets made by the Chitimacha Indians who live near the island. Today Harvard archaeologists from the Peabody Museum are conducting a dig on Avery Island, searching for evidence of prehistoric inhabitants.

Walter McIlhenny, president of the pepper sauce empire, notes that his grandfather's creation is now sold in ninety-two countries. The recipe for Tabasco calls for vinegar, salt, and crushed *Capsicum* peppers. These ingredients are listed right on the label, but the quantities — and the peppers — remain family property.

1868 OYSTER BISQUE

Serves 6

> 1 tablespoon lard or 2 tablespoons butter
> 2 tablespoons flour
> 1 large onion, finely chopped
> 1 quart boiling water (1 L)
> 4 dozen shucked oysters and their liquid
> 1 tablespoon butter
> 1 bay leaf
>   thyme to taste
>   salt to taste
>   Tabasco to taste
> 4 parsley sprigs, chopped

Melt the lard or butter in a large pot. Add the flour and blend thoroughly to form a roux. Add the onion and cook over medium heat until the mixture turns brown.

Add the boiling water, oysters and their liquid, butter, and bay leaf. Then add the thyme, salt, and Tabasco. Boil for 20 minutes. Remove half the oysters, let them cool, and chop them. Pass the soup and remaining oysters through a sieve. Reheat the soup with the chopped oysters. Garnish with chopped parsley.

1968 OYSTER BISQUE

Serves 6

> 2 10-ounce cans condensed oyster stew (57 dkg total)
> 3 cups milk (¾ L)
> ¾ cup water (1¾ dL)
> 2½ teaspoons dried minced onion
> 2 tablespoons dried celery flakes
> 2 bay leaves
> ½ teaspoon Tabasco
> 1 8-ounce can oysters, drained and chopped (23 dkg)
> 2 tablespoons flour
> 2 tablespoons water
> ¼ cup sherry (½ dL)
> 2 tablespoons dried parsley flakes

In a large pot, combine the undiluted oyster stew, milk, ¾ cup water, dried onion, celery flakes, bay leaves, Tabasco, and chopped oysters. Stir and bring to a boil. Reduce the heat and simmer for 10 minutes, stirring occasionally.

Combine the flour with 2 tablespoons water and blend until smooth. Stir this into the oyster stew mixture and simmer for another 2 minutes, stirring occasionally, until slightly thickened. Remove the pot from the heat and stir in the sherry. Garnish with parsley flakes.

Chilled Lobster Soup

Serves 6–8

When Burris Young shells out money for lobster, he always gets two meals from the investment. "First I serve boiled lobster to guests who aren't good at removing the meat," explains Young. "Preferably to people who do not wear lipstick. Then the shells are both meaty and clean — perfect for lobster soup."

Young's efficiency is demonstrated in his home and his office, both of which, it so happens, are in Massachusetts Hall. On the first floor of this administration building in Harvard Yard, Young is associate dean of freshmen. On the third floor, he lives in two ovenless suites. There Young has served as many as twenty guests from his hot plate and hibachi. Actually, he does most of his fancy cooking at his house on Cape Cod, where Young has a kitchen and a choice of fresh lobsters.

> shells from 4 1½–2-pound boiled lobsters (68–90 dkg)
> 1½ cups sherry (3½ dL)
> 3 bay leaves
> 3–4 cups chicken stock (¾–1 L)
> white pepper to taste
> ½–1 quart light cream (½–1 L)
> 2 tablespoons chopped fresh parsley

Remove the eyes from the lobster shells and discard them. Break the shells or cut them with scissors into 1-inch pieces. Break the legs at the joints and snap the claws if any remain intact. Place the shells in the smallest pot that will accommodate them, preferably a 2-quart (2 L) pot. Add the sherry and bay leaves. Add enough chicken stock to just cover the shells. Season with pepper.

Cover and cook over low heat for 2 hours, stirring and mashing the shells frequently, until the broth is flavorful and reddish-brown in color. Strain the soup and stir in the cream. Cover and refrigerate overnight. Before serving, whisk the soup and garnish it with the chopped parsley.

Seafood Soup Anisette

Serves 6–8

R ichard Rosen (Class of 1971) attended Harvard
during some tumultuous years. The intense political climate inspired him to write a "premature
memoir" entitled *Me and My Friends, We No Longer Pro-
fess Any Graces*. The book was a reflection of Rosen's cul-
tural indigestion and included such chapters as "Hot Sausage Links: An Allegory of American Politics" and "One
Entrecôte to Go, Easy on the Béarnaise: Food as People's
Art."

Rosen pursued his interests in cooking and current
events, respectively, as the restaurant critic for *Boston
Magazine* and as a reporter for the "Ten O'Clock News"
on WGBH, Boston's public broadcasting station.

He is also an avid and experimental cook. After produc-
ing his first batch of homemade gefilte fish, Rosen wondered what to do with its leftover component — fish stock.
He decided to use it as part of a soup, adding favorite
seafoods, from swordfish to mussels. The fish stock that
results from making *Love Story* Gefilte Fish (page 9)
serves as a fine base for Rosen's anise-flavored creation.

The galloping gourmet jumping over a quill-tipped pen is nineteenth-century food critic Charles Monselet. "Oeufs Monselet," the outrageously French egg dish that was devised in his honor, features artichoke hearts, chicken stock, veal nuggets, and cream sauce with sherry — topped with poached eggs and garnished with truffles. The recipe, along with the caricature by André Gill, can be found in Radcliffe's Dictionnaire de l'académie des gastronomes.

2 tablespoons butter
2 tablespoons olive oil
1 large, sweet red pepper, chopped
2 leek bulbs, chopped
¼ teaspoon powdered saffron
½ teaspoon thyme
1 bay leaf
  salt and pepper to taste
4 cups fish stock (1 L)
½ cup dry white wine (1 dL)
1½ pounds mussels, scrubbed (68 dkg)
1 pound haddock fillet, cut into 1-inch pieces (46 dkg)
½ pound swordfish, cut into 1-inch pieces (23 dkg)
½ pound scallops (23 dkg)
2–4 tablespoons Anisette liqueur
½ cucumber, peeled and thinly sliced
½ cup grated Parmesan (1 dL)

Heat the butter and oil in a large, heavy pot. Add the sweet red pepper and leeks and cook until they turn soft. Add the seasonings, fish stock, wine, and mussels. Cover and simmer for 2–3 minutes. Add the remaining seafood, liqueur, and cucumber. Cover and simmer for another 5–10 minutes, until the mussel shells open. Adjust the seasonings and remove the bay leaf. Sprinkle each serving with grated Parmesan.

Iroquois Roast Corn Soup

During the week of her graduation from Harvard's Graduate School of Education, Hazel Dean-John welcomed family members and other visiting well-wishers according to Iroquois tradition. She made a big pot of roast corn soup. At home it would have taken eighteen hours, using bushels of Indian corn and huge outdoor pots. In Cambridge she accelerated the process by using sweet corn and a stove.

As a "faith-keeper" (religious leader) for the Seneca nation of the Iroquois people, Hazel Dean-John is devoted to preserving Iroquois culture. She lives on the Allegheny Reservation in New York, where she is known for her woodcarving, bead work, basketweaving, and cooking. This corn and bean soup is rich and hearty, with smoky, salty flavors from the roasted corn and salt pork.

ONAHN-DAH

Serves 15–20

> 12 ears white Indian corn or sweet corn*
> 1 pound lean salt pork, diced (46 dkg)
> 1 pound cooked kidney beans and their liquid (46 dkg)
> ¼–½ cup dried corn (½–1 dL)*

Place the shucked corn on a griddle or in large, cast-iron skillets. Cook over low heat, turning the ears gradually, until the kernels are golden, about 30 minutes. The corn will make snapping noises and blacken in places. Remove the corn and let it cool.

Meanwhile, in a 5-quart pot, combine the beans' liquid with enough water to make 4 quarts (3¾ L). Add the salt pork and bring to a boil. Reduce the heat and simmer until the roast corn is ready. Using a sharp, heavy knife, scrape the corn kernels into a bowl. Add these kernels to the simmering liquid, along with the cooked kidney beans and dried corn. Simmer for 1 hour, stirring occasionally.

---

* On the reservation, Indian corn, with its large white kernels, grows from 12–26 inches long. Sweet corn makes an adequate substitute.
Instructions for making dried corn follow the recipes for onahn-dah.

QUICK ONAHN-DAH

Serves 12

When Hazel Dean-John is feeling particularly rushed, she makes a version of roast corn soup that takes even less time than the one preceding.

    2 1-pound cans whole kernel corn (90 dkg total)
    2 1-pound cans creamed corn (90 dkg total)
    1 1-pound can kidney beans (46 dkg)
    1 pound salt pork, diced (46 dkg)
    ¼ cup dried corn (½ dL)

Combine all ingredients in a large pot. Cover and simmer for 30 minutes.

DRIED CORN

Corn, squash, and beans are the "three sisters" of the Iroquois diet, and post-harvest preservation makes them staples year-round. Drying the corn is a time-honored ritual. When Dean-John explains that "you scrape the corn three times," the echo of generations is in her voice.

To begin the corn-scraping, shuck the corn and reserve the husks. An ear at a time, hold corn balanced on its end in a baking dish. Using a sharp knife, slice downward, cutting off the tips of each row of kernels. The second time, press the blade firmly against the cob, scraping the remaining kernel meat into the baking dish. During the final scraping, bear down hard against the cob, pressing as much "milk" as possible into the dish. Reserve the cobs.

Spread the corn evenly on the bottom of the dish and mash the kernels to release their milk. Bake at 350°F (180°C) for 45 minutes to 1 hour until corn is dried and brown. Scrape from the pan and store in glass jars. The Iroquois use dried corn in soups and casseroles, or as a snack. Dried corn is also good in omelettes and salads.

For the Iroquois, cooking is only one of many uses for corn. Dean-John converts the husks into masks for corn festivals and uses the cobs to make pipes and dolls.

Bol à bouillon *from* Le Livre de Cuisine, *a nineteenth-century cookbook in Radcliffe's Schlesinger Library.*

Minted Rice and Mushroom Soup

Serves 4

Fran Silverman, registrar at Harvard's Peabody Museum of Archaeology and Ethnology, makes travel arrangements for exhibits that will visit other cities. Many of these displays focus on the preparation and consumption of food and include cooking utensils and serving bowls from far-flung cultures.

Silverman notes that the Peabody Museum also offers various food-related programs, among them a seminar on the breadmaking of Native Americans. The staff members have documented their own culinary interests by compiling a book of their favorite recipes. Silverman's contribution is this pleasant soup, a minted refreshment for lunch or a light supper.

½ pound mushrooms (23 dkg)
3 tablespoons butter
2 onions, finely chopped
1 tablespoon flour
5 cups chicken stock (1¼ L)
  salt and pepper to taste
1 tablespoon uncooked rice
1 bay leaf
½ tablespoon chopped fresh mint or ½ teaspoon dried
  mint
½ tablespoon chopped fresh parsley or ½ teaspoon dried
  parsley

Remove the stems from the mushrooms and mince them. Thinly slice the mushroom caps. Melt 2 tablespoons of the butter in a pot. Add the onions and cook until they turn clear. Add the mushrooms, cover, and cook over low heat for 5 minutes. Remove the pot from the heat, add the remaining butter, and stir in the flour. Add the chicken stock, salt, and pepper, and return the pot to the heat. Bring the soup to a boil. Add the rice and bay leaf and stir. Reduce the heat and simmer for 15–20 minutes, until the rice is tender. Discard the bay leaf and adjust the seasonings. Add the mint and parsley, stir once, and serve.

Split Pea Soup with Caraway and Honey

Serves 6

Bob Goodman appreciates good food and good exercise. A doctoral candidate at the School of Education, he teaches emotionally disturbed children at a school outside Boston. In addition to more traditional subjects, he offers a class on vegetarian cooking.

Goodman finds that when students try recipes (like this vegetarian version of traditional pea soup), they gain experience in "language expansion, sensory integration, sequencing, and recall." The students may not understand the jargon, but they do like cooking and eating their lessons!

Still, Goodman expects them to work some of it off. He's also a member of the Radcliffe-Harvard Dance Company, and leads his students in physical exercise.

        2 tablespoons vegetable oil
        3 tablespoons butter
        4 large carrots, grated
        2 onions, finely chopped
       ½ cup chopped fresh parsley (1 dL)
        2 cloves garlic, minced
        1 pound dried split peas (46 dkg)
      2½ quarts water (2½ L)
        2 tablespoons honey
        1 tablespoon caraway seeds
          salt and pepper to taste
          croutons, sliced scallions, or chopped hard-boiled eggs
            for garnish

Heat the oil and butter in a 4-quart (4 L) pot. Add the carrots, onions, parsley, and garlic. Cook over medium heat for 5–10 minutes, stirring occasionally. Add the split peas and water, and bring to a boil. Reduce the heat, add the honey and caraway seeds, and simmer uncovered for 2 hours, stirring frequently. Season with salt and pepper. Allow the soup to cool to room temperature, then purée it in a blender or food processor. To serve, reheat and top each serving with one of the suggested garnitures.

Avgolemono

(Greek Egg-Lemon Soup)

Serves 6–8

When she was thirty-two, psychologist Matina Souretis Horner became the youngest president in Radcliffe's hundred-year history. Among her many functions as president, Horner oversees Radcliffe's Schlesinger Library on the History of Women in America; the Institute for Independent Study (a center for scholarship by and about women); and the Data Resource and Research Center (a base for social-science research on the lives of educated women). Horner is also an associate professor of psychology and social relations at Harvard and a consultant to the University Health Services.

A native Bostonian, Horner is known nationally for her "fear of success" studies on women's attitudes toward their careers. Those fearing success should avoid her family's recipe for avgolemono: it leads inevitably to a real achievement — a soothing and satisfying egg-lemon soup.

> 6 cups chicken broth or stock (1½ L)
> ½–1 cup uncooked long-grain rice (1–2 dL)
> 5 large eggs
> ½ teaspoon cornstarch
> 4–5 tablespoons lemon juice
>   salt and pepper to taste
>   lemon wedges

In a large pot, bring the broth to a boil. Add the rice, cover the pot, and simmer for 15–20 minutes, until the rice is tender. Break the eggs into a bowl and beat until frothy. Combine the cornstarch with ¼ cup (½ dL) of the hot broth and stir to blend thoroughly. Stir this mixture into the beaten eggs. Add the lemon juice and continue stirring. Pour 1 cup (¼ L) of the hot broth into the egg-lemon mixture, stirring constantly.

Remove the soup from the heat. Gradually add the egg-lemon mixture, stirring constantly. Let the soup stand for a few seconds. Season with salt and pepper. Serve with lemon wedges.

Black Bean and Celery Soup

Serves 8

Working at home has its advantages, including the chance to cook on the job. With black beans on simmer, free-lancer Barbara Gale (Class of 1970) edits books for Boston-area publishers, including Harvard University Press.

Gale's black bean soup, unlike most, is not puréed. It makes a full-bodied vegetarian entrée when served with bread, cheese, and salad.

    1 pound dried black beans (46 dkg)
    1 tablespoon bacon fat or margarine
    2 cloves garlic, minced
    3 onions, chopped
    3 celery stalks with leaves, chopped
    2 cups vegetable stock (½ L)
    1 teaspoon dried celery flakes
    ½ teaspoon salt
    ½ teaspoon pepper
    1 teaspoon lemon juice

Wash the beans and place them in a large bowl. Add enough water to cover the beans by at least 1 inch. Let them soak overnight.

Place the beans and the soaking water in a large pot with enough additional water to cover the beans. Bring to a boil over high heat. Reduce the heat, cover, and simmer for 2–2½ hours, stirring frequently, until the beans are tender.

Melt the bacon fat or margarine in a skillet. Add the garlic and onions, and cook over low heat until the onions turn clear. Add the celery, cover the pot, and cook for another 5 minutes. Add the contents of the skillet to the simmering beans, along with the vegetable stock, dried celery leaves, salt, pepper, and lemon juice. Bring the soup to a boil. Reduce the heat, cover, and simmer for 1–1½ hours, stirring frequently.

Serve the soup plain, or with garlic croutons, or with lemon wedges and sour cream.

Shaker Tomato Soup

Serves 8

The Shakers, so-named for their trembling during worship, have helped put the Divinity School on Cambridge's culinary map. Somewhere along the line, a Divinity School chef began serving Shaker dishes in the school's cafeteria. The recipes, passed on to succeeding chefs, are now in the hands of Margery Collins.

Collins, too, has helped make the Divinity School cafeteria one of the best spots for hot, winter lunches at Harvard. Each weekday she makes up a fresh batch of soup, which is sold at a modest price to some two hundred patrons in the know. A favorite, and an old standby, is this spirited soup with its perky flavor and sour cream topping. Collins serves it at least twice a month at Rockefeller Hall, 47 Francis Avenue.

> 7 pounds chopped fresh tomatoes (3¼ kg) or 4 1-pound cans stewed tomatoes with their liquid (180 dkg total) *
> 1 onion, chopped
> 2–3 celery stalks with leaves, chopped
> 1 green pepper, chopped
> 2 bay leaves
> 1–2 teaspoons basil
> 1 tablespoon salt
>   cayenne pepper to taste
> ½–1 tablespoon lemon juice
> 1–2 tablespoons sugar
> ½ cup sour cream (1 dL)
> 1 tablespoon chopped fresh parsley

In a large pot, combine the tomatoes, onion, celery, green pepper, bay leaves, and basil. Cover and simmer for at least 30 minutes, stirring and mashing occasionally. (If the mixture seems too thick, add a little water.) Add the salt, cayenne, lemon juice, and sugar. Bring the soup to a boil. Remove the bay leaves. Serve with a dollop of sour cream and a sprinkle of parsley.

* Some combination of fresh and stewed tomatoes may also be used.

Tomato-Yogurt Crew Soup

Serves 8

Before 1858, the Harvard crew and its opponents wore long white underwear during races. This made things difficult for fans on the river bank, who couldn't tell one ghostly crew from the other. The Back Bay Regatta of that year was a turning point. The Harvard stroke bought nine bright red bandannas, which he and his fellow crew members tied around their heads. At that race, Harvard fans cheered for the crimson, a practice that continues to this very day.

Radcliffe crew members, unlike their Harvard counterparts, race in black and white uniforms. Among them is Diana Shaw (Class of 1980), a varsity coxswain for Radcliffe's heavyweight crew, who weighs in at a mere 90 pounds. Light, nourishing foods like this cold crimson soup help keep her at the ideal coxswain weight.

> 1½ cups plain yogurt (3½ dL)
> 3 tablespoons lemon juice
> 1 tablespoon vinegar
> salt to taste
> 9 cups tomato juice (2¼ L)
> 1 tablespoon curry powder
> 2 cucumbers, chopped or sliced
> pepper to taste
> chopped fresh parsley for garnish

Beat the yogurt in a large bowl until it is smooth. Add the lemon juice, vinegar, and salt. Stir to blend thoroughly. Stir in the tomato juice. Add the curry powder, cucumber, and pepper. Cover and refrigerate for at least 4 hours. Garnish with parsley.

Harvard's early students enjoy a meal in their room in this illustration from the Harvard University Archives.

Curried Squash Soup

Serves 4–6

As a research fellow in visual and environmental studies at Harvard's Carpenter Center for Visual Arts, Bill Rothman teaches courses on film history and criticism. In the world of movies, his particular fascination is with Alfred Hitchcock, about whom he has written a book. In the world of gastronomy, however, he is a notorious fan of Indian cooking. Here is his recipe for a cold curried soup.

    1 small butternut squash, peeled, seeded, and chopped
    1 large onion, chopped
    2 cloves garlic, crushed
    2 tablespoons Indian curry powder

3 cups chicken or beef stock (¾ L)
3 tablespoons butter
   salt and pepper to taste
2 cups milk (½ L)

In a large pot, combine the squash, onion, garlic, curry powder, and stock. Bring to a boil. Reduce the heat, cover, and cook over low heat for 45 minutes. Remove the pot from the heat. Mash the mixture until it is smooth. Add the butter, salt, and pepper, stirring until the butter melts. Add the milk and stir to blend thoroughly. Serve the soup lukewarm or reheat it without boiling. If, as Rothman does, you prefer the soup cold, refrigerate it, covered, for 2 hours. Serve it plain or experiment with toppings like chopped parsley or cucumber, yogurt or sour cream.

Salads

[OVERLEAF] *Illustrations of salads are not easy to come by. This one appears in* The Royal Cookery Book, *by French chef Jules Gouffé. Taking advantage of "modern" printing techniques, Gouffé illustrated his cookbook with 161 woodcuts from drawings by E. Ronjat.*

Gado-Gado

(Indonesian Steamed Vegetables
with
Peanut Sauce)

Serves 4

Algae-rakers, fin-snatchers, mollusk-crushers, larvae-smashers. This list, which reads like a WANTED poster of aquatic sadists, describes the eating habits of cichlids (pronounced *"sicklids"*), a highly competitive family of freshwater fish. Cichlids have evolved teeth of various shapes and sizes that enable them to exploit virtually every food in their waters.

Karel Liem, who is the Henry Bryant Bigelow Professor of Ichthyology, studies dental diversity in these successful scavengers, but he and his family have more discriminating taste. This fresh, colorful salad is Indonesian, like Liem. The accompanying peanut sauce, also used on chicken kebabs, is flavored with coconut milk and lime juice. Gado-gado looks nice on a circular tray, a wheel of rich gifts for the eye and the palate.

THE SALAD

    1 8-ounce package bean sprouts (23 dkg)
    2 cups green beans, cut into 1-inch pieces (½ L)
    2 cups shredded cabbage (½ L)
    2 cups sliced zucchini (½ L)
    2 hard-boiled eggs, sliced
    1 cucumber, sliced
 8-10 colored shrimp chips, fried *

Steam separately for 2–3 minutes the bean sprouts, green beans, cabbage, and zucchini. (Other nonsweet vegetables, such as green peppers and lettuce, may also be used.) Let them cool to room temperature and place them in piles on a circular tray. Decorate with sliced egg and cucumber, and fried shrimp chips.

THE SAUCE

    1 onion, finely chopped
    1 clove garlic, minced
  1-2 dried red peppers
    1 tablespoon brown sugar
    2 tablespoons margarine
    1 12-ounce jar creamy peanut butter (34 dkg)
    2 cups unsweetened coconut milk (½ L)†
    1 lime

Place the onion, garlic, red pepper, and brown sugar on a flat surface and mash them until they form a paste. (Liem uses two flat stones for this procedure.) Melt the margarine in a large, deep skillet. Add the onion mixture and cook over low heat for 2–3 minutes. Add the peanut butter and stir to blend thoroughly. Pour in a little of the coconut milk, raise the heat slightly, and stir to blend

---

* Shrimp chips are sold in Oriental markets.
† Unsweetened coconut milk can be found in Oriental, Latin, and gourmet shops, or can be processed from fresh coconuts.

thoroughly. Continue adding coconut milk a little at a time, stirring constantly to blend, until all the milk is used and the sauce thickens as it comes to a boil. This should take about 15 minutes.

Remove the sauce from the heat. Grate the peel from the lime and add it to the sauce. Squeeze the lime juice into a cup (discarding the seeds) and stir it into the sauce. Let cool to room temperature. Serve as a sauce for the steamed vegetables.

Liem also serves gado-gado with chicken kebabs that have been basted with some of the peanut sauce. This recipe makes enough sauce to do both.

Soap Opera Salad with Dilly Sour-Cream Dressing

Makes 2 cups of dressing

Students love to conjecture about life after graduation in the proverbial "real world" they've heard so much about. When actress Laurie Heineman graduated from Harvard in 1971, she chose to enter *Another World* instead. In this television soap opera, Heineman played Sharlene, and earned an Emmy for outstanding performance.

Heineman lived in New York City while working on the soap and followed the summer traffic to Fire Island for escape. There she acted out the following scenario:

Scene 1. Arrive late Saturday morning with assorted friends and groceries. Quickly combine sour cream with dried onion soup. Dip raw vegetables into the mixture while drinking red wine and preparing a supper of lamb.

Scene 2. Late that afternoon make a salad dressing using dill, onion dip, sour cream, and wine. Pour the dressing over a salad made with some of the remaining vegetables and serve it alongside the lamb.

Scene 3. Sunday noon, remake the salad dressing with all appropriate leftovers. Finely chop the vegetables and lamb that remain. Stuff them into pita bread and top with the dressing. Sunday afternoon, head back to Another World.

    2 tablespoons onion dip
    ½ cup sour cream (1 dL)
    ¼ cup plain yogurt (½ dL)
    3 tablespoons lemon juice
    1 teaspoon grated lemon peel
    1 tablespoon wine vinegar
      splash red wine
    1 tablespoon Dijon mustard
  3–4 tablespoons chopped fresh dill or 1 tablespoon dried
      dill
      salt and pepper to taste

Combine all the ingredients and adjust flavors to taste. Pour over chopped vegetables: carrots, celery, cucumber, tomatoes, cauliflower, broccoli, zucchini.

Broccoli and Olive Salad

Serves 6–8

Students who have passed through Harvard Law School in recent years may remember this salad from the Harkness Common cafeteria. The credit goes to Rachael Raven, food services manager for this stu-

Legumes from Jules Gouffé's Le Livre de Cuisine, *published in Paris in 1867. The book is now housed at Radcliffe's Schlesinger Library.*

dent facility and other dining areas for Law School faculty and staff.

Cooks at Harkness Common prepare the salad in quantity, and Raven scales it down in her kitchen for guests. Generally, however, she avoids catering at home. After planning menus all week, she prefers to spend weekends taking company *out.*

> 2 pounds fresh broccoli, cut into 1-inch pieces (90 dkg)
> 2 celery stalks, scraped and cut into ¼-inch pieces
> ½ cup chopped pimiento-stuffed green olives (1 dL)
> 2 scallions, sliced
> ½ cup mayonnaise (1 dL)
> 3 hard-boiled eggs, finely chopped

Steam the broccoli until it is just tender. Place the broccoli in a bowl, then refrigerate until cool. Add the celery, olives, scallions, and mayonnaise. Toss gently and top with the chopped eggs.

In this drawing and collage from Harvard's Busch-Reisinger Museum, nineteenth-century German artist Adolf Oberlaender whimsically imposes a deli ad over characters from a children's story.

German Potato Salad with Sweet-Sour Dressing

Serves 4–6

Art from central and northern Europe adorns Harvard's Busch-Reisinger Museum, a baroque building complete with sculpture garden and clock tower. The Busch-Reisinger is known for its expressionist, Bauhaus, and Renaissance art works. It also houses a large collection of eighteenth-century porcelain dishes and an impressive Flentrop organ played by noted guest musicians. As membership and development officer for the museum, Emmy Dana manages museum press tours and conferences and edits a newsletter publicizing concerts and shows.

Dana's knowledge of German culture goes back to the culinary arts she learned as a child. Among the traditional recipes that her parents brought with them from Germany is this one for potato salad. The sweet-sour sauce used with the salad, says Dana, is just as delicious served over green beans.

THE SALAD

> 6 potatoes, peeled and cut into ¾-inch pieces
> 6 strips bacon
> 1 onion, finely chopped
> 2 tablespoons chopped fresh parsley

Boil the potatoes in salted water until tender. Meanwhile, fry the bacon until crisp and drain it on paper towels. Crumble the bacon and set it aside. Cook the chopped onion in the bacon grease until it turns clear. Remove the onion with a slotted spoon and set it aside. When the potatoes are tender, drain them and place them in a large serving bowl. Add the chopped parsley, onion, and bacon bits. Toss gently and cover to keep warm.

THE DRESSING

  1 tablespoon flour
  ½ cup water (1 dL)
  ½ cup vinegar (1 dL)
  2–4 tablespoons sugar
  1 teaspoon salt

Combine all ingredients in a saucepan. Bring to a boil over high heat, stirring constantly, and boil for 1 minute. Pour the sauce over the potato salad. Serve warm.

Revitalized Waldorf Salad

Serves 4

As a ghost-writer and sometimes ghost-chef, Richard Steadman (Class of 1971) has worked on various cookbooks, including one that offers cooking as a form of psycho-therapy.

Devising topical variations on standard fare is a regular part of Steadman's profession. Here's his "health food" version of the perennial Waldorf, spruced up with cashews, lime juice, and sprouts.

  1 cup firmly packed alfalfa sprouts (¼ L)
  ½ cup raw cashews, chopped (1 dL)
  ⅓ cup currants or raisins (¾ dL)
  ⅓ cup plain yogurt (¾ dL)
    juice of 1–2 limes
  3 Newton or Pippin apples, peeled and chopped

Combine all the ingredients in a large bowl and toss. Cover and refrigerate until ready to serve. If the apples are chopped early in the procedure, squeeze the lime juice over them immediately to delay discoloration.

Moroccan Chili-Tomato Salad with Lemon Juice Dressing

Serves 4

After a summer of travel in Morocco, Ann Coles returned with a pair of new recipes. The first one is for this assertive salad with finely chopped vegetables, North African style. The companion recipe of honey-flavored lamb stew, appears on page 190. Coles, a graduate student at the School of Education, serves them together to make a complete Moroccan meal.

THE SALAD

　　1 4-ounce can green chilis, finely chopped (16 dkg)
　　2 large tomatoes, seeded and finely chopped
　　⅓ cup chopped fresh parsley (¾ dL)

THE DRESSING

　　2 tablespoons lemon juice
　　3 tablespoons olive oil
　　　pinch ground cumin
　　　pinch crushed fennel or anise seed
　　　salt to taste

Combine the salad ingredients in a bowl. In a small bowl, mix together the ingredients for the dressing. Toss the salad with the dressing.

Tabulee Salad

Serves 4

A salad that doubles as an hors d'oeuvre, this Middle East mixture features wheat, mint, and lemon. Bob Collins, sales manager for the Harvard University Printing Office (HUPO), serves it to complement an entrée of lamb or, with small loaves of pita, as an appetizer at dinner parties. He garnered the recipe from his Lebanese in-laws, who supplement the standard parsley with crisp, shredded lettuce.

Collins works at the HUPO facility in Boston, located a short walk from Harvard Stadium. There he helps coordinate 12,000 printing jobs yearly, including such projects as Harvard diplomas and menus.

> 1 cup borghul wheat (¼ L) *
> ½ cup finely chopped Italian parsley (1 dL)
> ½ cup finely chopped mint leaves (1 dL)
> 1½ cups shredded lettuce (3½ dL)
> 4–5 scallions, minced
> 2 tomatoes, finely chopped
> juice of 1 lemon
> ¼ cup vegetable oil (½ dL)
> salt to taste

Soak the borghul in water for 2 hours. Drain, and squeeze out as much moisture as possible. In a large bowl, combine the borghul with the remaining ingredients. Mix thoroughly before serving.

* Also known as bulgar, this ingredient is available in Middle Eastern markets and natural-foods stores.

Tuna Louie

Serves 4

Haymarket, Boston's liveliest outdoor fruit and vegetable market, is particularly busy around closing time when shoppers can bargain for very ripe produce. Harvard ecologist Paul Hertz made a good deal one summer afternoon when he traded ninety cents for a case of soft avocados. After that, Hertz really had to eat fast. When he discovered that he was out of mayonnaise, he promptly mixed avocado with his tuna.

As an ecologist, Hertz has a soft spot for animals and that matches his regard for the environment. He buys only tuna that says "Albacore" on the label. Other tunas, he explains, share their waters with dolphins, which are killed inadvertently during tuna fishing.

Hertz, who shares his home with a boa constrictor and three flying squirrels, is grateful to the Museum of Comparative Zoology, his home away from home while completing his thesis. With a nod to the museum and its founder, Louis Agassiz, Hertz now blends avocado and tuna on purpose.

> 2 7-ounce cans Albacore tuna, drained and flaked (40 dkg total)
> 2 ripe avocados
> 5 scallions, minced
> 1 celery stalk, finely chopped
> 1 tomato, finely chopped
> 4 teaspoons lemon juice
> ½ teaspoon garlic powder
> ½ teaspoon Hungarian paprika
>   hot pepper sauce
>   salt and pepper to taste

Place the tuna in a large bowl. Slice the avocados in half lengthwise and remove the pits (which can be saved, rooted, and planted). Scoop the avocado meat into the bowl. Mash it while mixing with the tuna. Add the remaining ingredients and stir to mix thoroughly. Hertz enjoys the mixture as a salad by itself, stuffed into tomatoes, or in a sandwich.

Curried Shrimp and Peanut Salad

Serves 8–10

J udith Parker is an associate editor of *Harvard Magazine,* which is circulated to 185,000 alumni and other interested readers. Many of the magazine's readers are writers themselves, so Parker edits a column spotlighting books by alumni. She also edits a reading guide that surveys various bodies of literature, and she matches story ideas with appropriate writers.

Parker's knack for finding the right combination is also evident in the kitchen. While organizing the menu for a dinner party, she came up with this bright idea. First she paired the flavors of shrimp and curry. Adding peas for color and peanuts for texture, Parker created this fine curried coleslaw.

THE SALAD

    1 medium cabbage, grated
    3 4½-ounce cans tiny, cooked cocktail shrimp, drained
    1 cup dry-roasted peanuts (¼ L)
    1 cup cooked peas, drained (¼ L)

THE SAUCE

  1 **cup sour cream** (¼ L)
  1 **cup plain yogurt** (¼ L)
  1 **cup mayonnaise** (¼ L)
5–7 **tablespoons curry powder**

In a large bowl, combine the ingredients for the salad and toss. Prepare the dressing, adding curry powder (and possibly salt) to taste. Pour the dressing over the salad and stir to mix thoroughly. Cover and refrigerate for at least 2 hours. Before serving, sprinkle a little curry powder on top for color.

Lobster and Avocado Salad

Serves 2–4

As a curatorial associate of the Harvard Theatre Collection, Martha Mahard directs the use of dramatic ephemera. The vast collection, stored in the Pusey Library, includes posters and playbills, scene and costume designs, and even the menu from a George M. Cohan testimonial dinner.

Mahard's enthusiasm for the theater and theater history is matched by her interest in murder mysteries and cooking. The fictional Nero Wolfe, a gourmet detective, left clues for this fresh lobster salad while sleuthing his way through *A Window for Death*.

Pantomime prints, which sold for a "penny plain, tuppence colored," were popular in Britain during the nineteenth century. Plain ones were preferred by children, who colored them in. This print is now part of a gathering of theatrical portraits tended by Martha Mahard at the Harvard Theatre Collection.

1 ripe avocado, peeled and sliced
¼ cup dry white wine (½ dL)
2 teaspoons tomato paste or ketchup
½ teaspoon prepared horseradish
¾ chopped dates (1¾ dL)
1 tablespoon chopped chives
2 scallions, minced
  lemon juice to taste
  salt and pepper to taste
2 cups cooked lobster meat (½ L) *

Place the avocado slices in a bowl with the wine. Cover and refrigerate while preparing the rest of the salad. In a bowl, combine the tomato paste, horseradish, mayonnaise, chives, and scallions. Add lemon juice, salt, and pepper. Add the lobster meat and stir to mix thoroughly.

To serve this elegant salad, arrange lettuce leaves on a platter and mound the lobster salad on top. Sprinkle with paprika. Place the avocado slices on or around the salad. Garnish with parsley.

Jamaican Coleslaw

Serves 6–8

A globetrotter and former Peace Corp worker in Kenya, George Rosen (Class of 1968) has experienced a variety of cultures. When he isn't traveling, he can be found in his Cambridge apartment, writing novels that take place in India and Africa.

Recently Rosen vacationed in Negril, Jamaica, where

* A 2½-pound lobster (1¼ kg) yields about 2 cups of meat (½ L). Boiled lobster shells may be used to make Chilled Lobster Soup (page 39).

Mr. GRIMALDI, as CLOWN

An 1811 pantomime print featuring Mr. Grimaldi as Clown in Harlequin and Asmodeus, *performed at London's Theatre Royal Covent Garden. The print is part of the Harvard Theatre Collection at Pusey Library.*

he frequented a restaurant owned by a Jamaican man and a French woman. The establishment served this lively island coleslaw with a tart topping of French vinaigrette. The combination suited Rosen's tastes precisely. His version is nestled amid Boston lettuce.

> 4 cups shredded cabbage (1 L)*
> 2 cups shredded carrots (½ L)
> 1 cup cooked corn, drained (¼ L)
> 1 cup roasted peanuts (¼ L)
> ½ cup raisins (1 dL)
> ¾ cup vinaigrette (1¾ dL)*
> 2 hard-boiled eggs, sliced
> 2 tomatoes, sliced
> ⅔ cup grated cheddar cheese (1½ dL)
> 6–8 leaves Boston or other lettuce

In the center of a large, deep serving dish, arrange layers of cabbage, carrots, corn, peanuts, and raisins. Pour on most of the well-mixed vinaigrette. Decorate the surface with sliced hard-boiled eggs and tomatoes. Top with grated cheddar cheese. Tuck the lettuce leaves around the edges of the serving platter. Drizzle the remaining vinaigrette over the lettuce.

* One small head of cabbage should yield this amount.

A recipe for vinaigrette can be found in a French or good basic cookbook.

Breads, Muffins, and Popovers

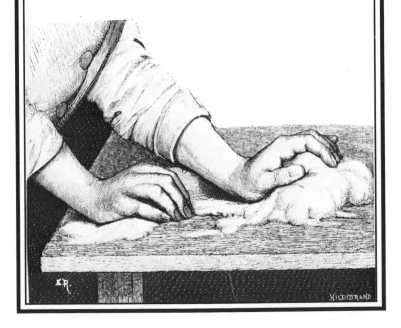

Bathtub Bread

Makes 2 loaves

B ecause his kitchen lacked counter space, physics lecturer Jay Blake used to knead dough in his bathtub. One time Blake made a dough that just wouldn't rise. He tossed the disaster back into the tub and went off to vent his frustration at Harvard's Gordon Mc-Kay Lab. On returning, Blake made a pleasing discovery. A friendly fungus had consumed the flour's gluten and released carbon dioxide to raise the dough.

This cleaned-up version of Blake's bathtub experiment, complete with hints on kneading, baking, and controlling the crust, translates the art of bread-baking into a fine science. Because it makes use of refrigerated risings, this recipe suits the busy schedules of physicists and other cooks.

4 tablespoons butter
1 cup milk (¼ L)
1 tablespoon sugar
½ tablespoon salt
1 cup cool water (¼ L)
1 package yeast
6 cups sifted flour (1½ L)
  butter

In a saucepan, combine the butter, milk, sugar, and salt. Cook over low heat until the butter melts. Pour the mixture into a large bowl, add the cool water, and let stand for several minutes. Add the yeast. Gradually stir in about 4½ cups (1¼ L) of the flour, mixing until well blended. Turn the dough out onto a floured surface and let it stand for 10 minutes. Gradually add the remaining flour and knead vigorously for 10–15 minutes until the dough is smooth and satiny.

Put the dough in a lightly floured bowl, cover it tightly, and place it in the refrigerator for at least 2 hours, until it has doubled in size. (You *can*, Blake points out, leave it there overnight. If enough heat has been transferred from the hands to the dough during kneading, the yeast will accomplish a 2-hour rising regardless of how much additional time the dough is refrigerated.)

Remove the dough, punch it down, and turn it out onto a floured surface. Knead it until it is warmed to a satiny texture again. Replace it in the flour-dusted bowl, cover it, and refrigerate for at least 2 more hours.

Remove the dough, punch it down, and turn it out onto a floured surface. Divide the dough in half, form two loaves, and place them in lightly greased 5-by-9-inch loaf pans. If your oven heats slowly, place the loaf pans in the cold oven and set the temperature at 350°F (180°C). The loaves will accomplish the third rising before baking. *Or* cover the loaves and let them rise for another 2 hours.

Just before baking, make several 1-inch diagonal cuts across the top of each loaf and drop in pieces of butter. Bake at 350°F (180°C) for 45 minutes. For a thick crust, use an atomizer to spray water on the surface several times during baking.

Cinnamon Raisin Bread

Makes 2 loaves

When Bill Liller wishes upon a star, he is most likely considering what makes it so bright. Liller, the Robert Wheeler Wilson Professor of Applied Astronomy, studies the variation of brightness in stars. "I focus on stars in a globular cluster," he explains. "That means a gathering that is smaller than a galaxy."

Liller's research is based at the Harvard College Observatory, but he prefers to stargaze from a quiet mountain top. This pastime, says Liller, always leads to the munchies. That's one of the reasons he learned to cook. Another good reason is his wife, Martha, with whom he shares mountain tops and kitchen responsibilities.

Martha Liller is curator of the observatory's astronomical photographs. The collection, referred to by astronomers around the world, provides an almost continuous record of what the sky looked like from 1890 clear through last night.

In addition to their common fascination with the skies, the Lillers share a fondness for homemade bread. Thus, these heavenly loaves were developed — for consumption by starlight or less romantic illumination.

2 cups warm water (½ L)
1 package yeast
2 teaspoons salt
6 cups sifted flour (1½ L)
1 cup raisins (¼ L)
½ cup sugar (1 dL)
1–2 teaspoons cinnamon
    butter

Preheat the oven to 150°F (66°C). In a large bowl, combine the warm water, yeast, salt, and 4 cups (1 L) of the flour. Stir to blend thoroughly. Gradually add the remaining flour. Turn the dough out onto a floured surface and knead for 5–10 minutes, until it is smooth and elastic. Turn off the oven.

Place the dough in a greased, heat-resistant bowl, turning so the grease coats all the dough's surface. Place the bowl in the warm oven, above a pan of hot tap water. (This procedure is designed to help keep the dough moist.) Let it rise for 1 hour or until double in bulk.

Punch down the dough and turn it out onto a floured surface. Divide the dough in half and use a rolling pin to roll each section into a flat rectangle. Sprinkle each piece with half the raisins, sugar, and cinnamon. Roll up each piece like a jelly roll, tucking in the filling at the ends and pinching the dough together to secure the loaf. Place the loaves in greased 5-by-9-inch loaf pans. Return them to the warm oven, positioned above a new pan of hot water. Let them rise for 1 hour and then remove them from the oven.

Heat the oven to 400°F (205°C). Leave the pan of water in the oven and bake the loaves for 20 minutes. Dot the top of each loaf with butter and continue baking for another 10–15 minutes.

Nutmeg Challa

Makes 2 loaves

H arvard has the largest university library in the world and the oldest in this country. The headquarters of this bibliographic commonwealth is Widener Library, where Maria Hurley catalogues books in English, Spanish, and German.

Although her rich, braided bread comes from a Jewish, Eastern European tradition, Hurley classifies it with recipes for Christmas baked goods. She also distinguishes her challa with nutmeg, a fragrant addition to each golden slice.

    1 package yeast
 1¼ cups warm water (3 dL)
    2 cups boiling water (½ L)
    3 tablespoons vegetable oil or softened butter
    1 tablespoon salt
  ⅓ cup sugar (¾ dL)
  ¼ teaspoon nutmeg
    2 eggs, beaten
    8 cups sifted flour (2 L)
    1 egg yolk, beaten
    2 teaspoons poppy seeds

Mix the yeast with the warm water and set it aside. In a large bowl, combine the boiling water, oil, salt, sugar, and nutmeg. Stir to blend thoroughly. Add to this the 2 beaten eggs and the yeast mixture. Gradually stir in the flour. Turn the dough out onto a floured surface and knead for 10 minutes, until it is smooth and satiny. Place the dough in a greased bowl, cover it with a towel, and let it rise for 1 hour or until doubled in bulk. Punch it down, cover it, and let the dough rise for another hour. Turn it out onto a floured surface, punch it down, and divide the dough in half.

Separate each half into 3 equal parts. Roll each of the pieces into sausagelike strips about 12–16 inches long. Place them side by side on greased cookie sheets. Cover the dough strips with a towel and let them rise for 1 hour.

Braid each group of 3 strips into a loaf, pinching the ends together and tucking them under. Brush the top of the loaves with the beaten egg yolk. Sprinkle the poppy seeds on top. Bake for 1 hour at 350°F (180°C), until golden brown.

God showers the Israelites with manna from heaven in this enthusiastic woodcut from a sixteenth-century Bible. The tome, published in Lyons, is part of the rare book collection at the Divinity School's Andover-Harvard Theological Library.

Whole Wheat Challa

Makes 2 loaves

DuTo the phase of Harvard history now referred to as the "period of unrest," some undergraduates with more moderate views than *The Harvard Crimson*'s founded a second newspaper on campus. *The Harvard Independent*, born in 1969, established an "open" editorial policy and welcomed articles from all members of the University community.

Today the weekly tabloid is known for its analytical features and extensive coverage of the arts around Harvard. Although it is less political than it was at its founding, the *Independent* still strives for varied perspectives by maintaining a diverse and independent staff.

As freewheeling in the kitchen as she is in editorial board meetings, associate editor Carey Sassower (Class of 1979) bakes these unconventional challas. They have all the beauty of the traditional braided loaves, with the added full flavor of fresh, whole wheat bread.

```
        2 packages yeast
        ⅔ cup warm water (1½ dL)
        ⅔ cup lukewarm milk (1½ dL)
        ¼ cup honey (½ dL)
        2 sticks butter, melted
        3 eggs, lightly beaten
  5½–7 cups whole wheat flour (1¼–1¾ L)
        2 teaspoons salt
     2⅔ teaspoons baking powder
        1 egg
        1 tablespoon milk or water
```

In a small bowl, combine the yeast and warm water. Let the mixture stand for 5 minutes. In a large bowl, combine the lukewarm milk and honey. Stir into this mixture the butter and the 3 beaten eggs. Add the yeast mixture and stir to blend thoroughly.

Sift together the flour, salt, and baking power. Sift this gradually into the previous mixture. Stir to blend thoroughly. Turn the dough out onto a floured surface and knead for 10–15 minutes until it is smooth. Place the dough in a greased bowl, turning so the grease coats all the dough's surface. Cover the dough with a towel and let it rise in a warm place for 1½–2 hours, until doubled in bulk.

Punch down the dough, turn it out onto a floured surface, and divide it in half. Separate each half into 3 or 4 equal parts. Roll each of these into sausagelike strips. Braid each group of 3 or 4 strips into a loaf, pinching the ends together and tucking them under.

Place the loaves on greased cookie sheets. Cover them with a towel and let them rise in a warm place for 1 hour. Beat the remaining egg with the milk or water. Brush this mixture on top of the challas. Bake at 350°F (180°C) for 45–50 minutes.

Abstract Expressionist Bread

Makes 2 loaves

This bread is rather flat, but it's loaded with energy. That's how Louis J. Bakanowsky came up with its name, and why he once sent a loaf to painter Robert Motherwell.

As a professor of architecture (at the Graduate School of Design) and of visual and environmental studies (at the Carpenter Center), Bakanowsky easily finds parallels between breads and buildings: he knows what quality he wants from the finished product and builds with the finest materials. This healthful construction is toasted for Bakanowsky's breakfast. It fills him and keeps him designing for hours.

>   4 cups whole wheat flour (1 L)
> 1½ cups gluten flour (3½ dL)*
>   2 cups cracked wheat (½ L)
>   1 cup coarse, unprocessed bran (¼ L)
>   1 cup wheat germ (¼ L)
>   2 teaspoons sea salt
>   2 packages yeast
>   1 cup warm water (¼ L)
> ⅔ cup honey (1½ dL)

In a large bowl, combine the flours, cracked wheat, bran, wheat germ, and salt. Stir to blend thoroughly. Dissolve the yeast in the warm water and add it to the flour mixture. Add the honey and stir to blend thoroughly. Beat in a bread mixer or turn out onto a floured surface and knead for 5–8 minutes.

Place the dough in a bowl, cover it with a towel, and let it rise in a warm place for 30 minutes. (Don't expect it to increase *too* much.) Punch down the dough, turn it out onto a floured surface, and knead it for another 5 minutes.

Divide the dough in half and place in greased 5-by-9-inch loaf pans. Cover the dough and let it rise in a warm place for 1 hour. Bake at 375°F (190°C) for 50 minutes.

* Gluten flour is often sold in natural foods stores; so are most of the other ingredients, such as bran, wheat germ, and sea salt.

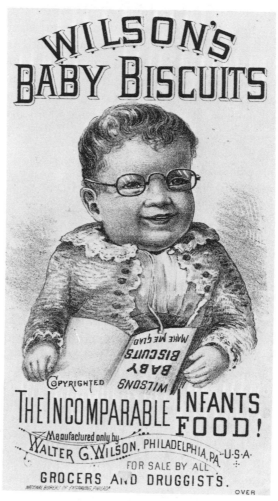

Trade cards, the predecessors of modern American business cards, were abundant in this country toward the end of the nineteenth century and grew in popularity with the rise of lithography. The Baker Library of Harvard's Graduate School of Business Administration houses a large collection of early American trade cards, including this one. These biscuits, according to the information on the back of the card, "are easy of digestion . . . Infants cry for them . . . Invalids greatly relish them."

Gold Medal Dinner Rolls

Makes about 30

The only United States hockey team to earn the Olympic gold medal had four Harvard alumni playing full force. The team, which triumphed at Squaw Valley in 1960, was led by Bill Cleary, forward wing and high scorer. Cleary is a native Cantabrigian who played hockey as a Harvard undergraduate. He now coaches the University's varsity team, which has battled competitively in recent NCAA playoffs.

Diet, says Cleary, plays a role in team performance. Players meet at the Varsity Club about five hours before game time. There they chow down on steak, pancakes, and eggs, supplemented with tea and a selection of juices.

At the end of the season the senior players are invited to feast at Cleary's home. Bill and his wife, Jo, follow this recipe for rolls because it produces thirty per batch. Hockey players, the Clearys report, tend to put away four rolls apiece.

7–7½ cups sifted flour (1¾–2 L)
½ cup sugar (1 dL)
2 packages yeast
2 teaspoons salt
1 stick butter or margarine, softened
2 cups hot tap water (½ L)
1 egg
vegetable oil

In a large mixing bowl, combine 2¼ cups (½ L) of the flour with the sugar, yeast, salt, and softened butter or margarine. Gradually add the hot tap water, beating with an electric mixer until the yeast is dissolved and the mixture is smooth. Add the egg and continue beating. Gradually beat in another ¾ cup (2 dL) flour or enough to make a thick batter. Continue beating for another 2 minutes.

Gradually add another 3½ cups (8 dL) flour and stir by hand to form a soft dough. Turn the dough out onto a well-floured surface and knead for 10 minutes, adding more flour as needed, until the dough is smooth and elastic. Place the dough in a large, lightly greased bowl, turning so the grease coats all the dough's surface. Cover the dough with a towel and let it rise in a warm place for 1½ hours or until doubled in bulk.

Punch down the dough and push the edges to the center. Turn it over and brush lightly with a little vegetable oil. Tightly cover the dough with plastic wrap and refrigerate it, punching it down occasionally until ready to use. The dough may be refrigerated for up to 7 days.

Handfuls of dough may be removed as desired to make fresh rolls each day of the week. To bake all the dough at once for the full 30 rolls, divide the dough in half and roll 15 balls from each half. Place the balls in a single layer in greased baking pans. Cover them with a towel and let them rise in a warm place for 1½ hours or until doubled in bulk.

Bake the rolls at 425°F (220°C) for 15 minutes, until golden brown. Brush the tops with melted butter or margarine. Serve warm.

Rum Date-Nut Muffins

Makes 2 dozen 2-inch muffins

D uring the school year Lorraine G. Cummings
serves lunch and dinner to the four hundred students who live in Eliot House. She is melancholy
in June when the house empties out, but summer brings a
new set of responsibilities at Harvard. Tossing aside her
Food Services apron, she swings into duty for Buildings
and Grounds, working as a substitute for custodians on
vacation.

One summer Cummings was stationed at Wadsworth
House in Harvard Yard (where George Washington
worked — and slept — during the New England mobili-
zation). Currently the headquarters for the Associated
Harvard Alumni, Wadsworth House has a kitchen, which
made Cummings nostalgic. When her nurturing instinct
got the better of her, Cummings began showing up early
for work. She baked these rum muffins with exquisite
timing. They made a warm morning welcome for the in-
coming staff.

   1¾ cups sifted flour (4 dL)
    ¾ teaspoon salt
    2 teaspoons baking powder
    ¼ cup brown sugar (½ dL)
    ¼ cup white sugar (½ dL)
    ¾ cup chopped dates (1¾ dL)
    ½ cup chopped walnuts (1 dL)
    2 eggs, beaten
   .3 tablespoons butter, melted
    ½ cup milk (1 dL)
    5 tablespoons rum

Sift together the flour, salt, and baking powder. Add the brown and white sugar, dates, and walnuts. In a small bowl, combine the beaten eggs with the melted butter, milk, and rum. Stir to blend thoroughly. Add this to the flour mixture and stir briefly, leaving some lumps. Pour the batter into greased muffin tins until each cup is ¾ full. Bake at 400°F (205°C) for 20–25 minutes.

Harvard Club of New York Popovers

Makes about 2 dozen

U pstairs, members enjoy traditional hospitality at the Harvard Club in New York City. A barber, bootblack, masseur, and resident cat provide all the comforts of home, and then some. Club spectators work up a lather watching reruns of Harvard football games, while athletes keep cool playing air-conditioned squash.

Afterward, members choose among several dining areas and sip coffee from oversized "Teddy Roosevelt cups." (A member of the Class of 1880 and a former club officer, Roosevelt complained that the second cup of coffee never lived up to the first. The club obliged by combining the two.)

Downstairs in the kitchen, baker Juan Lugo perpetuates another of the club's great traditions — popovers. His recipe, translated from Spanish, comes with one culinary confession: when the club's commercial oven overheats, the popovers don't puff. This recipe, adapted to accommodate smaller ovens, *should* provide popovers in perfect form.

  5 eggs
  1 quart milk (1 L)
  1½ tablespoons salt
  3⅓ cups sifted flour (8 dL)

Whisk the eggs and half the milk in a large bowl. Add the salt. Gradually add the flour and the remaining milk, beating until smooth. Pour the batter into well-greased muffin or popover tins. (Lugo recommends using vegetable shortening.) Bake at 450°F (230°C) for 15 minutes. Reduce the temperature to 350°F (180°C) and continue baking for another 20 minutes.

These popovers, a standard feature on all Harvard Club tables, are served with butter and orange marmalade.

Boston Brown Bread

Makes 1 loaf

One of the easiest ways to be creative at Harvard is to sign up for Jacki Braun's studio art course. Offered under the auspices of Harvard's Office for the Arts, her course is free, has no prerequisites, and is open to employees and students alike.

Braun, a native New Englander who teaches drawing, painting, and sculpture, is also proficient in the culinary arts. Authentic New England cooking is nearly a lost art in her opinion. Braun does her part to preserve a great culinary tradition with this classic recipe for Boston brown bread.

CUISINE
ARTISTIQUE

*Frontispiece from the two-volume classic by Urbain Dubois.
The richly illustrated treatise, published in Paris in 1883, is
now housed at Radcliffe's Schlesinger Library.*

1 cup rye meal or flour (¼ L)
1 cup corn meal (¼ L)
1 cup graham flour (¼ L)
¾ teaspoon baking soda
1 teaspoon salt
1 egg, lightly beaten
¾ cup molasses (1¾ dL)
2 cups sour milk or buttermilk (½ L)
1 cup raisins

Combine the dry ingredients in a large bowl. Add the egg, molasses, and milk, stirring until smooth. Add the raisins and stir. Pour the batter into a greased 5-by-9 inch loaf pan. Bake at 350°F (180°C) for 1 hour.

Officer Fennelly's Irish Bread

Makes 1 round loaf

The Harvard University police force originated in the seventeenth century, when a Cambridge constable and six guards protected Harvard Yard. Police and Security today consists of seventy members, including Lawrence Fennelly on the crime prevention team. Fennelly provides the University with tips on safety — from parking lot lighting to pedestrian routes home from evenings at Widener Library. Officer Fennelly's roots can be traced back to Ireland, where his grandmother learned to make this sweet bread.

      2¼ cups sifted flour (5½ dL)
      2¼ teaspoons baking powder
      ⅛ teaspoon salt
      ¾ cup sugar (2 dL)
      ¼ cup vegetable oil (½ dL)
      1 large egg, lightly beaten
      ¾ cup milk (2 dL)
      1 cup raisins (¼ L)
      1 tablespoon caraway seeds

Combine the dry ingredients in a large bowl. Add the remaining ingredients and stir to mix thoroughly. Turn out onto a floured surface and knead to form a smooth dough. Place the dough in a greased and floured circular 9-inch cake pan and shape into a round loaf. Bake at 350°F (180°C) for 45–50 minutes.

Hearth Bread

Makes 1 loaf

C arol Dornbrand likes supper to be as relaxing as possible. Queuing up with four hundred students simply isn't her style. That's why Dornbrand (Class of 1980) settled in a Jordan Cooperative instead of in one of Harvard's twelve residential "houses." Each of the three Jordan Co-ops, located behind Radcliffe Quadrangle, houses no more than thirty undergraduates who share the responsibility for planning and preparing meals.

Jordan members appreciate the nutritious fare and informal living. So do their friends. Frequently co-op cooks wind up feeding guests from the other housing facilities who gladly abandon another cafeteria-style supper for real down-home cooking in a cozy environment.

When Dornbrand takes her turn in the co-op kitchen, she bakes this hearth bread with a vegetarian entrée. Like many of the co-op cooks, she shuns white flour and sugar in favor of whole grains and honey.

2½ cups whole wheat flour (6 dL)
1 teaspoon baking soda
1 teaspoon baking powder
1 teaspoon salt
  cinnamon to taste
½ cup honey (1 dL)
¼ cup vegetable oil (½ dL)
1½ cups buttermilk (3½ dL)
½ cup chopped walnuts (1 dL)
1 tablespoon grated orange rind

In a large bowl, sift together the flour, baking soda, baking powder, and salt. Season with cinnamon. Stir in the remaining ingredients and blend to form a smooth batter. Pour the mixture into a greased 5-by-9-inch loaf pan. Let it stand for 20 minutes. Bake at 375°F (190°C) 45 minutes to 1 hour.

Pumpkin Bread

Makes 2 loaves

Class reunions are held just once a year, but Jane Opel (Class of 1950) spends all twelve months setting the stage. As a Radcliffe administrator for alumnae affairs, Opel prepares for the one thousand alumnae who arrive in Cambridge each year during commencement week. Opel, who plays the hostess and the trouble-shooter while the show is underway, of course also makes an appearance at her own class reunion.

Then, when the event is over, Opel rewards herself and her staff by baking pumpkin bread and bringing it to work. By the time the moist treat has been devoured, it's time to get started on next year's production.

    3 cups sugar (¾ L)
    1 cup corn oil (¼ L)
    4 eggs, beaten
    1 1-pound can pumpkin (46 dkg)
 3½ cups sifted flour (8 dL)
    1 teaspoon baking powder
    1 teaspoon baking soda
    2 teaspoons salt
  ½ teaspoon cloves
  ½ teaspoon ginger
    1 teaspoon cinnamon
    1 teaspoon nutmeg
    1 teaspoon ground allspice
  ½ cup water (1 dL)
  ¾ cup chopped walnuts (2 dL)
    1 cup raisins (¼ L)

In a large bowl, combine the sugar, oil, eggs, and pumpkin, stirring to blend thoroughly. Sift together the flour, baking powder, baking soda, salt, and spices. Gradually add this to the pumpkin mixture alternately with the water. Add the nuts and raisins and stir to mix thoroughly. Pour the batter into two lightly greased and floured 5-by-9-inch loaf pans. Bake at 350°F (180°C) for 1 hour or until a toothpick inserted into the center comes out clean. Serve the bread with butter or cream cheese.

This pumpkin was submitted by Theresa Muñoz (Class of 1981) for a beginning drawing class at the Carpenter Center for the Visual Arts. Muñoz, who is concentrating in visual and environmental studies, takes many of her classes at the center, the only building designed by Le Corbusier in North America.

Almond–Poppy Seed Loaf

Makes 1 loaf

A congressional representative from Colorado, Pat Schroeder is the first woman to serve on the House Armed Services Committee. Her belief that we spend too much money on arms got her into trouble with F. Edward Hébert (pronounced ā-bāre), the former chairman of that committee. Schroeder made herself even more visible in Washington by wearing a button that read HELP! I HAVE A BEAR BY THE TAIL!

Schroeder and her husband, Jim, studied law together at Harvard. Their lives are hectic: two careers, two children, and two homes (Washington and Denver). Nonetheless, they budget time for home cooking. This quick bread, nice with brunch or afternoon tea, infringes very little on their schedules.

1¼ cups sugar (3 dL)
1 cup evaporated milk (¼ L)
1 cup vegetable oil (¼ L)
2 eggs, lightly beaten
1 teaspoon almond extract
1 teaspoon baking powder
¼ teaspoon salt
2 cups sifted flour (½ L)
¼ cup poppy seeds (½ dL)

In a large bowl, combine the sugar, milk, oil, eggs, and almond extract. Add the baking powder and salt. Gradually add the flour, mixing to form a smooth batter. Stir in the poppy seeds. Pour the batter into a lightly greased and floured 5-by-9-inch loaf pan. Bake at 375°F (190°C) for 1 hour.

Eggs, Pasta,
and Vegetables

[OVERLEAF] *Boiled eggs from* The Royal Cookery Book *by Jules Gouffé. The book, published in London in 1883, is part of the culinary collection at Radcliffe's Schlesinger Library.*

Fruit Liqueur Omelette

Serves 2

If you're looking for an excuse to drink wine for breakfast or simply deserve a luxurious morning, try this omelette with a bottle of German Auslese or Spätlese. Such are the recommendations of Fred and Cynthia Smith, who lace their omelette with cherry or orange liqueur and top it with dollops of liqueur-flavored whipped cream.

The Smiths are wine importers who own Cave Atlantique, a Harvard Square wine store with six hundred choices. Fred (Class of 1962) and Cynthia (Law School 1969) note that their wines range from $2 to $100, although most of their business comes from purchases of $6 and under. The white wines they mention to accompany this omelette can be purchased for around $10.

THE TOPPING

  ½ pint heavy cream, whipped (¼ L)
  1 tablespoon maraschino or orange liqueur

THE OMELETTE

  3 eggs
  3 tablespoons heavy cream
  3 tablespoons maraschino or orange liqueur
  1 tablespoon blueberry or strawberry jam
     butter

To make the topping, gently fold the tablespoon of liqueur into the whipped cream. To make the omelette, lightly mix the eggs with the heavy cream and liqueur. Use this mixture to make an omelette in your preferred way.

Lightly butter the finished omelette and make a narrow incision along its length. Spoon a thin line of the jam along this incision. Place the omelette on a serving platter. Spoon three dollops of the flavored whipped cream over the omelette. Serve with white wine.

Author Jules Gouffé puts all his eggs in one basket in this woodcut from Radcliffe's copy of The Royal Cookery Book.

Nobel Frittata

Serves 6

T he Academy in Sweden recognized George Wald for his work on the biochemistry of the eye. Harvard students remember him for his introductory science course, Natural Sciences 5, which Wald taught until his retirement as Higgins Professor of Biology. Ruth Hubbard (Class of 1945, Ph.D. 1950), who wrote her senior honors thesis under Wald's direction, knows him also as the chef who bakes this Italian omelette. Now a Harvard professor of biology herself, Hubbard is Wald's partner in both marriage and research.

> 2 10-ounce packages fresh or frozen, chopped spinach (57 dkg total)
> salt
> 2 tablespoons olive oil
> 1 onion, finely chopped
> 1 large clove garlic, minced
> oregano to taste
> basil to taste
> salt and pepper to taste
> 5 eggs
> ½ cup grated Parmesan or Romano, or crumbled feta (1 dL)
> ½ cup milk (1 dL)

If using fresh spinach, sprinkle the leaves with salt and tear them into 2-inch pieces. Let the leaves stand for several minutes. Then rinse them, squeeze out the water, and place them in a large bowl. *Or* defrost the frozen spinach, drain it, and place it in a large bowl.

Heat the olive oil in a skillet. Add the onion and garlic.

Season with oregano, basil, salt, and pepper. Cook over medium heat until the onion turns clear. Add the contents of the skillet to the spinach and mix thoroughly. Beat the eggs in a separate bowl. Add the cheese and milk to the beaten eggs and continue beating until well mixed. Stir this into the spinach-onion mixture.

Pour the mixture into a greased 9-by-9-inch or 9-by-12-inch baking dish. Bake at 350°F (180°C) for 20–25 minutes until the frittata has set and is light brown on top.

Wald serves this dish hot as a main course, or allows it to cool, cuts it into squares, and serves it with toothpicks as an hors d'oeuvre. He varies the recipe by substituting 1 pound (46 dkg) sliced mushrooms for half the spinach, or by adding chopped peppers and other vegetables.

Poached Eggs with Spinach and Artichoke Hearts

Serves 2

T he Harvard Extension School, founded at the turn of the century, offers several degree programs and nearly three hundred courses. It is staffed largely by Harvard faculty, and most classes are held in the evening so that working people can continue their educations.

Jamie Forrester is an advocate of continuing education, and to further the cause he has sampled courses in writing and politics. His independent efforts include a medley of careers, from cab driver to banjo picker in a traveling country-western band.

Forrester's tastes are as varied as his experience. One of

his favorite breakfasts is an eclectic dish of lamb kidneys fried with onions, mushrooms, and wine, and topped with a fried egg. In complete contrast is this elegant special-occasion brunch recipe, which requires a delicate touch and a good sense of timing.

> 1 cup cooked spinach, drained and chopped (¼ L)
> ¾ cup sour cream (1¾ dL)
> 6–8 cooked artichoke hearts, halved
> 2 English muffins, split and toasted
> 4 poached eggs
> 1 cup Hollandaise sauce (¼ L)

In a saucepan, combine the spinach, sour cream, and artichoke hearts. Warm over low heat. Spoon the mixture over the toasted English muffin halves and top with poached eggs. Drizzle a narrow ribbon of Hollandaise sauce on top. Or, says Forrester, skip the Hollandaise altogether. Without it, this dish is still very rich.

This lone artichoke appears in the chapter on vegetables in The Royal Cookery Book, *published in London in 1883. The book is one of several by Jules Gouffé in the cookbook collection at Radcliffe's Schlesinger Library.*

"Agaricus rodmani. *In grass by Charles River, Cambridge, Mass. Oct. 1906." Harvard botanist W. G. Farlow commissioned several artists over twenty years to make illustrations of New England fungi. This drawing, now found in the library of Harvard's Farlow Herbarium, comes from Louis C. C. Krieger, a part of that team.*

Spinach-Stuffed Manicotti in Mushroom White Sauce

Serves 4–6

W hile busloads of schoolchildren and other visitors peer at the dinosaur bones and stuffed animals in the Museum of Comparative Zoology, archivist Ann Blum works above the hubbub, on the second floor. There, in a small room in back of the museum's library, Blum catalogs diaries, field notes, and scientific drawings from many of the great nineteenth-century naturalists (see page 209). She is also gathering material for a book on natural-history illustration, gleaning some of the art from the museum's own collection.

Blum and a friend invented this spectacular dish on a dreary Sunday afternoon. It takes a while to prepare and dirties plenty of dishes, but with four hands the work is a pleasure.

12 no. 66 manicotti noodles
    salt
 3 tablespoons olive oil
 1 large onion, finely chopped
 1 clove garlic, pressed
1¼ cups cooked spinach, drained and chopped (3 dL)
 1 pound ricotta cheese (46 dkg)
 2 eggs, lightly beaten
    salt and pepper to taste
 ½ pound mozzarella cheese, thinly sliced (23 dkg)
 8 tablespoons butter
 2 cups thinly sliced mushrooms (½ L)
 5 tablespoons flour
 2 cups milk, heated (½ L)
 1 cup prosciutto cut into julienne strips (¼ L)
 2 tablespoons chopped fresh parsley
 ¾ cup grated Parmesan (1¾ dL)
    fresh or dried parsley, oregano, or basil

Cook the manicotti in boiling salted water for 4 minutes. Drain in a colander and slide gently into a bowl of cool water.

Heat the olive oil in a skillet. Add the onion and garlic and cook over low heat until the onion turns clear. In a large bowl, combine the onion and garlic with the cooked spinach. Add the ricotta, eggs, salt, and pepper, stirring to mix thoroughly. Gently stuff the manicotti with the spinach-ricotta mixture and arrange them in a greased baking dish. Cover with the mozzarella slices.

Melt 3 tablespoons of the butter in a skillet. Add the mushrooms and cook until they turn soft. Make 2 cups of white sauce by melting the remaining butter in a saucepan and stirring in the flour to form a roux. Add the heated milk and whisk over low heat until the sauce thickens. Remove the sauce from the heat. Add to the white sauce the mushrooms, prosciutto, and parsley.

Pour the sauce over the stuffed manicotti and sprinkle the grated Parmesan on top. Bake at 375°F (190°C) for 20–25 minutes, until the cheese is melted and the sauce is bubbling. Garnish with parsley, oregano, or basil.

Sicilian Spaghetti with Patriotic Sauce

Serves 6

The flag of Italy is red, white, and green, just like this spaghetti dish from Palermo, Sicily. The patriotic recipe came to America around the turn of the century with Alfred Panepinto's mother. Panepinto, a 1931 graduate of the School of Design, adapted some details but left the basic plan intact. The result is a rich, red tomato sauce, dotted with meatballs and bright green peas.

THE SAUCE

 2 28-ounce cans tomato purée (1½ k total)
 1 tablespoon chopped fresh parsley
 1 tablespoon oregano
 1 tablespoon salt
 ⅓ teaspoon pepper
  pinch of sugar
 ¼ cup olive oil (½ dL)
 3 onions, finely chopped
 3 cloves garlic, minced
 ¼ cup red wine (½ dL)
 1 10-ounce package frozen peas (29 dkg)

In a large pot, combine the tomato purée, parsley, oregano, salt, pepper, and sugar. Simmer over low heat. Meanwhile, heat the olive oil in a large skillet. Add the onions and garlic, and cook until the onions turn golden. Add the wine, cover, and simmer for 1–2 minutes. Add the onion mixture to the simmering sauce. (Note that the peas are added later, about 5 minutes before serving.)

THE MEATBALLS

 1 pound lean ground beef (46 dkg)
 ½ pound sweet Italian sausage meat, removed from the
   casing (23 dkg)
 3 onions, finely chopped
 3 cloves garlic, minced
 1 egg, lightly beaten
 ¾ cup dried bread crumbs (1¾ dL)
 ¼ cup milk (½ dL)
 2 teaspoons chopped fresh parsley
 1 teaspoon oregano
 1 tablespoon grated Romano
  salt and pepper to taste

Combine the ground beef and sausage meat in a large bowl. Gradually add the remaining ingredients and stir to mix thoroughly. Roll the mixture into balls the size of large olives. Brown the meatballs in a skillet over low heat. Drain them on paper towels and add them to the simmering sauce. Cover the sauce and simmer for another 2 hours, stirring occasionally. Just before serving, add the frozen peas. Cover and simmer for 3–5 minutes, until the peas are tender.

Panepinto adds a time-saving suggestion for people who don't want to roll dozens of meatballs: Make a meat sauce by browning the ground beef and sausage meat in a large skillet, along with the suggested amount of chopped onions and garlic; drain the mixture and add it to the simmering sauce.

THE PASTA

    1 **pound no. 9 spaghetti (46 dkg)**
    2 **tablespoons salt**

Cook the spaghetti in boiling salted water, stirring occasionally, until tender. Drain the spaghetti in a colander and rinse briefly with hot water. Serve the spaghetti with the tomato and pea sauce, accompanied by red wine, which fits in with the color scheme.

Lampoon Eggplant

Serves 4

The Harvard Lampoon began its history of shenanigans in 1876, when seven student pranksters published an irreverent rag. *The Harvard Lampoon, or Cambridge Charivari, Illustrated, Humorous, etc.* is still being published as *The Harvard Lampoon*. Contemporary "Poonies" launch this literary assault from an actual fortress, the Lampoon Castle, located behind Holyoke Center, Harvard's main administration building. The magazine often aims ridicule at *The Harvard Crimson,* but few Harvard institutions or personalities have escaped some insult.

Not all the club's gestures are derogatory, however. In 1976 the Lampoon awarded a purple and gold Eldorado Cadillac, a trip to Las Vegas, and $10,000 to Harvard economist John Kenneth Galbraith, winner of the "Funniest Professor of the Century" contest. The club also sponsors free cultural events, such as the spring "Lawn-Care Equipment Concert," which features Poonies in tuxedos playing lawn mowers and hedge shears.

The Lampoon contribution to this Harvard cookbook comes, allegedly, from Admiral Elmer Green, caretaker of the castle for over half a century. Mitchell Pross, Lampoon president in 1978, claims, "Green was convinced that the eggplants were battleships. He supplied them with a garnish of national flags and toy soldiers." More likely the recipe is Pross's creation, along with the tall tale about Admiral Green.

(113)

"Poonie" T. K. Chang (Class of 1977) used his artistic skills to embellish the menu for an historic Lampoon dinner.

2 small eggplants
½ cup olive oil (1 dL)
2 cloves garlic, minced
1 large onion, finely chopped
1 green pepper, finely chopped
  grated rind of 1 lemon
2 tablespoons lemon juice
  salt and pepper to taste
4 tablespoons butter, melted
½–1 cup grated Parmesan (1–2½ dL)

Cut the eggplants in half lengthwise. Scoop out and coarsely chop the eggplant pulp, leaving the skins intact. Heat most of the olive oil in a large skillet. Add the eggplant pulp and cook over medium heat until soft.

Meanwhile, heat the remaining olive oil in a separate skillet. Add the garlic, onions, and green pepper, and cook until the pepper turns soft. Combine the eggplant with the onion–green pepper mixture. Add the lemon rind, lemon juice, salt, and pepper. Stir to mix thoroughly.

Spoon the mixture into the four eggplant skins and place them in a large, greased baking dish. Pour the melted butter on top of each eggplant and sprinkle the grated Parmesan on top. Bake at 375°F (190°C) for 35 minutes.

Tomato Frost Casserole

Serves 4–6

Organic gardener Marjorie B. Cohn cooks this casserole with green tomatoes that have been foiled by frost. Her skills at salvaging damaged materials are also displayed at the Fogg Art Museum, where she restores paintings and teaches art conservation. Cohn's recipe has been shared with many Cambridge gardeners who face a short New England growing season. For those who don't garden, ripe tomatoes work, too, making an equally hearty tomato entrée.

　1　strip bacon *or* 2 tablespoons butter
　1　large onion, coarsely chopped
　4　cups coarsely chopped green tomatoes (1 L)
　4　cloves garlic, minced
　½　teaspoon dried red pepper
　½　teaspoon oregano
　　　salt to taste
　¼　cup sour cream (½ dL)
　½　cup grated cheese (1 dL)
　½　cup fresh bread crumbs (1 dL)
　2　tablespoons butter, softened

Fry the bacon in a large pot or casserole that can go from stove top to oven. Drain the bacon, crumble it, and set it aside. Remove all but 1 teaspoon of bacon fat from the pot. (*Or* melt the 2 tablespoons butter in the pot.) Add the onion and cook over medium heat until it turns clear. Stir in the tomatoes, garlic, red pepper, oregano, salt, and bacon bits. Cover and cook over medium heat, stirring occasionally, until the tomatoes are just tender. Add the sour cream and half the cheese. Stir to mix thoroughly and remove the pot from the heat.

In a small bowl, combine the remaining cheese, bread crumbs, and butter. Spread this mixture over the casserole. Bake at 350°F (180°C) for several minutes until the crumbs are golden brown and the cheese is melted.

Indian Vegetable Croquettes

Serves 4

Pragna Mehta, a Harvard research assistant from India, conducts renal research at the Peter Bent Brigham Hospital, where she performs experiments with chick embryos and rabbit aortas.

Not surprisingly, Mehta prefers vegetarian cooking, including these Indian deep-fried croquettes. The ingredients are an unusual assortment of vegetables, lime juice, and ginger, which combine to form a tantalizing blend. Mehta spices things up with a little hot pepper, but even without it there is plenty of flavor.

2 potatoes, peeled and coarsely chopped
2 carrots, peeled and sliced
2 cups frozen peas (½ L)
1 small onion, finely chopped
2 tablespoons lime juice
1 teaspoon minced fresh ginger
1 hot green pepper, finely chopped
1 tablespoon sugar
  salt to taste
1 egg, lightly beaten
⅔ cup dried bread crumbs (½ dL)
4 cups vegetable oil (1 L)

Boil the potatoes, carrots, and peas in water until they are tender. Drain them and mash them in a large mixing bowl. Add the chopped onion, lime juice, ginger, hot pepper, sugar, and salt. Stir to mix thoroughly. Shape the mixture into oval cutlets about 3½ inches long. Dip them first in the beaten egg, then in the bread crumbs.

Heat the oil in a large, deep skillet. Fry the cutlets for several minutes per side until they are golden brown. Drain them on paper towels. As an entrée, they may be served plain or with rolls and ketchup. As a side course, this recipe makes 8 servings.

Fiddlehead Ferns in Cheese Sauce

Serves 4

Ferns are the focus of Alice Tryon's life. An associate curator in Harvard's Gray Herbarium, she conducts research on fern biology and evolution. Tryon wears fern-patterned jewelry, sleeps on fern-patterned sheets, and drinks from fern-patterned glasses. Naturally, she also eats ferns when she can.

In spring Alice and her husband, Rolla (professor of biology and curator of the herbarium), scan New England for fiddleheads — the coiled young fronds of a variety of ferns. The Tryon's look in moist woods, on damp hillsides, and along railroad tracks where rainwater drains. They take just one or two from a plant (to aid its chances for survival), clipping the spiral tops just where they stop curling. They eat some fresh — in soup, salad, or sauce — then freeze some so they may taste spring all year round.

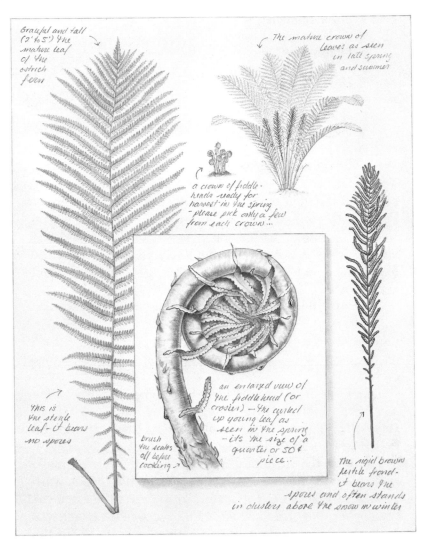

Graceful and tall
(2' to 5') the
mature leaf
of the
ostrich
fern

The mature crown of
leaves as seen
in late spring
and summer

a crown of fiddle-
heads ready for
harvest in the spring
- please pick only a few
from each crown...

this is
the sterile
leaf - it bears
no spores

brush
the scales
off before
cooking

an enlarged view of
the fiddlehead (or
crosier) - the curled
up young leaf as
seen in the spring
- its the size of a
quarter or 50¢
piece..

The rigid brown
fertile frond -
it bears the
spores and often stands
in clusters above the snow in winter

These drawings by scientific illustrator Sarah Landry provide
seasonal views of Matteuccia struthiopteris, commonly known
as the "ostrich fern." A contributing editor of Harvard Magazine and a consumer of fiddleheads herself, Landry also provided illustrations for the controversial Sociobiology (by Harvard professor Edward O. Wilson) and has done various
scientific renderings for the Museum of Comparative Zoology.

3–4 dozen fiddleheads*
2 tablespoons butter
2 tablespoons flour
1 cup milk (¼ L)
1 cup grated cheese (¼ L)
   lemon juice to taste
   salt and pepper to taste
4 English muffins, split and toasted

Wash the fresh fiddleheads, removing the brown scales. To prepare the cheese sauce, melt the butter in a saucepan. Add the flour and stir over low heat for 3–5 minutes. Pour on the milk and whisk until the sauce is thick and smooth. Remove the saucepan from the heat. Add the cheese and stir until it is completely melted. Stir in the lemon juice and season with salt and pepper. Cover and keep warm.

Place the fiddlehead buds in a shallow pan and add water to cover. Boil 3–12 minutes, depending on the tenderness desired. Drain the fiddleheads and arrange them on toasted English muffin halves. Spoon the cheese sauce on top.

The Tryons also serve boiled fiddleheads with lemon and butter, with boiled young carrots, and with boiled, tiny white onions. For a cold snack, they recommend boiled fiddleheads with a mayonnaise dip.

To freeze the fresh fiddleheads, place the washed buds in a shallow pan with water to cover. (The Tryons warn against adding salt to the water. This tends to blacken the buds when they are defrosted and recooked.) Bring to a boil and then remove the pan from the heat. Drain the fiddleheads, pat them dry, and place them in plastic containers before freezing.

* Fiddleheads flourish elsewhere in this country and across Canada in habitats similar to the ones described above. They may also be purchased in cans from some gourmet shops or by mail order from W. S. Wells and Son, Box 109, Wilton, Maine 04294.

Broccoli Pie

Makes a 9-inch pie

Robin Feibus (Class of 1979) manages the publishing division of Harvard Student Agencies, Inc., an organization that provides students with part-time jobs. Feibus hires other undergraduates to research, write, and edit the Agencies' annual series of *Let's Go* travel guides to Europe. A section of each book reviews the cuisine of the country, explaining how and what to order and what prices to expect.

Feibus herself provided some culinary copy about coffee houses in Cambridge for *The Unofficial Guide to Life at Harvard,* another of the Agencies' annual guide books. When she is in the mood for more private entertainment, she makes arrangements to cook in the Dunster House kitchen. There Feibus prepares this enticing broccoli pie, which she serves as an entrée at small dinner parties or as a snack at larger gatherings.

> pastry for a 9-inch lattice-top or double crust pie
> 2 tablespoons butter
> 1 cup sliced mushrooms (¼ L)
> 2 onions, finely chopped
> 3 cups cooked, chopped broccoli, drained (¾ L)
> 2 eggs, beaten
> ¾ cup grated Swiss, Gruyère, or cheddar cheese
> (1¾ dL)
> salt and pepper to taste

Bake the bottom pastry in the pie plate at 350°F (180°C) for 10 minutes. Remove the pie plate and let it cool, leaving the oven on.

Melt the butter in a skillet. Add the mushrooms and

onions, and cook until the onions turn clear. In a large bowl, combine the mushroom-onion mixture with the broccoli, eggs, and cheese. Add salt and pepper to taste. Stir to mix thoroughly. Pour the mixture into the pie shell. Top with the lattice strips or the full second crust, trimming and crimping the edges to form a sealed border. If using a full top crust, make 4 or 5 slits in the dough. Bake for 45 minutes, until set.

Cabbage-Apple Casserole

Serves 8

T his is a theme dish," explains journalist Fred Hapgood (Class of 1963). "It's meant to be adapted to the ingredients at hand." The core of his casserole is cabbage cooked in milk, but he offers a long list of other suggestions.

Hapgood, as flexible as his casserole, has written on everything from education to insurance. He has also been a science writer at the Harvard news office and has written a scientific book with a classic theme. Sex is the subject of his comprehensive treatise, from amoeba to zebra, with variations galore.

    2 cups sliced cabbage (½ L)
    2 cups sliced apples (½ L)
    2 cups sliced potatoes (½ L)
    1 large onion, sliced
    3 tablespoons butter
      salt and pepper to taste
    2 cups light cream or milk (½ L)
    ⅓ cup dried bread crumbs (¾ dL)
    1 cup grated Gruyère or cheddar cheese (¼ L)

Butter a large baking dish. Arrange in layers the cabbage, apples, potatoes, and onion, dotting each layer with butter and seasoning with salt and pepper. Pour on the cream or milk.

Cover and bake at 350°F (180°C) for 40 minutes. Uncover and sprinkle with bread crumbs and grated cheese. Return the casserole to the oven or place it under the broiler for several minutes until the surface is golden brown and the cheese is melted.

Variations on this theme: use pears or other noncitrus fresh fruits in place of the apples; use dried fruits such as apricots, raisins, or pineapple; add diced bacon or fillets of cod or haddock.

Information Casserole with Squash and Tomatoes

Serves 6–8

If you're looking for the phone number of Harvard's Project on Human Sexual Development, or a listing for the Map Collection, or the office number for Professor David Riesman, try calling Joan Nilson at 495-1000.

A telephone operator for Harvard's information lines, Nilson provides information on a host of subjects. She tells prospective students where to call for applications and advises vacationing tourists on exhibits at Harvard museums. She also helps those who are familiar with the University. Nilson once told an absent-minded professor which day school was to begin. During football season she accommodates out-of-state sports nuts who call her each hour to find out the score.

After work Nilson answers to the needs of her family. Her substantial summer casserole of squash and tomatoes is one of their favorite vegetarian repasts.

3 summer squashes, sliced
3 zucchini, sliced
1 onion, chopped
1 1-pound can stewed tomatoes, drained and chopped (46 dkg)
 salt and pepper to taste
 oregano to taste
1 cup grated Parmesan (¼ L)

Place all ingredients except the cheese in a large baking dish. Bake at 350°F (180°C) for 45 minutes. Sprinkle the grated Parmesan on top. Continue baking for another 5–10 minutes, until the squash is tender and the cheese is melted.

Fennel with Scallions

Serves 4

Arthur Maass, the Frank G. Thomson Professor of Government, is a specialist on "water law" and on the management of water resources. For Maass, aquatic interests go beyond professional boundaries. He was a resident of Boston's waterfront area long before it was considered chic, and his Atlantic Avenue penthouse offers a fine view of Boston Harbor.

With the wharf at his doorstep and the Italian North End at his back, Maass enjoys fresh fish and vegetables all year. In the Italian markets Maass was introduced to *finocchio* (fennel), which he now serves to complement seafood and lamb.

    4 cups sliced fennel (1 L) *
    ⅓ cup olive oil (¾ dL)
    1–3 cloves garlic
    ¼ cup minced scallions (½ dL)
        salt and pepper to taste

Trim the green ferny tops from the fennel and cut the stalks into 1-inch pieces. Heat the olive oil in a skillet. Add the garlic, cook it until brown, and then discard the clove. Add the fennel and cover. Cook over low heat 5–15 minutes, depending on the tenderness desired. Add the scallions and cook for 5 minutes, stirring occasionally. Season with salt and pepper. A garnish of grated orange rind is nice with this dish.

Harvard-Radcliffe Beets

Serves 6

As far as anyone around Cambridge can figure, Harvard beets are so-named for their crimson color. But what other colors *are* there for beets? Perhaps "Harvard" refers to the accompanying sweet-sour sauce. In that case, Radcliffe deserves equal time in the title. Since 1977, Harvard and Radcliffe have formally joined forces to provide food, housing, and education for all undergraduates.

The culinary component of the Harvard-Radcliffe

---

* Fennel has a bulbous bottom and a green fernlike top. It is known for its licorice perfume and flavor.

merger is headed by Frank Weissbecker, director of food services. Weissbecker supervises twenty kitchens and twenty-six dining halls at Harvard and Radcliffe residences and at several graduate schools. Also part of his domain is a network of underground tunnels near the Charles River. These passageways are traveled by a small band of electric trucks, which shuttle soup and baked goods from the central kitchen in Kirkland House to food-preparation areas in the four other "river" houses.

Weissbecker, who isn't crazy about beets of *any* name, agreed nonetheless to provide the traditional recipe. This version, adapted from the one in his files, uses fresh beets that are seasoned with mustard and caraway.

> 2½ pounds fresh beets with tops (68 dkg)
> ½ cup sugar (1 dL)
> 1 tablespoon cornstarch
> ¾ teaspoon salt
> ½ cup cider vinegar (1 dL)
> ¼ teaspoon dry mustard
> ¾ teaspoon crushed caraway seeds

Trim the beets of their green, leafy tops. (Like spinach, these can be steamed or boiled and served with butter or vinegar.) Wash the beets thoroughly and boil them in water until they are tender. Remove the beets and let them cool. Reserve ¼ cup (½ dL) of the cooking liquid.

Remove and discard the beet skins and chop or slice the beets. Cover them and keep them warm. Combine the remaining ingredients, including the reserved beet juice, in a large, heavy saucepan. Cook over a low heat, stirring constantly, until the sauce thickens as it comes to a boil. Reduce the heat, add the beets, and simmer for several minutes until they are well heated.

Broccoli-Cream Cheese Bake

Serves 4

Graduates of Harvard Business School are destined for financial success, earning an average of $25,000 their first year out of Harvard. But what is their success rate outside the office? Are high-powered careers and good marriages compatible? To improve the odds, Dr. Barrie Greiff, a psychiatrist at the Business School, offers "The Executive Family." The first course of its kind at an American graduate school, it is popular among Business School students and their mates. Greiff helps the couples to plan for the impact of success and to balance priorities between business and family.

Two-career marriages offer additional challenges and opportunities, as Greiff knows firsthand. His wife, Carole, is an interior designer who fashioned, among other things, the dining room at Boston's new Harvard Club. Sharing domestic responsibilities is part of their theory for success, and the Greiffs try to practice what they preach. This broccoli casserole is a joint enterprise that is appreciated by their three children.

    2 cups cooked chopped broccoli, drained (½ L)
    4 hard-boiled eggs, sliced into rounds
    1 3-ounce package cream cheese, softened (85 g)
    ¾ cup milk (1¾ dL)
      salt and pepper to taste
    2 tablespoons butter, melted
    ⅓ cup dried bread crumbs (¾ dL)

Place the cooked broccoli in a greased baking dish. Arrange the slices of hard-boiled eggs on top. Combine the cream cheese and milk in a saucepan and cook over a low

(127)

heat, stirring constantly, until smooth and thick. Season with salt and pepper. Pour the sauce over the broccoli and eggs. Combine the melted butter with the bread crumbs and sprinkle this on top. Bake at 350°F (180°C) for 30 minutes.

Fried Tomatoes Dusted with Politics

Serves 2–4

S tore-bought tomatoes can be dangerous weapons, according to Senator Adlai Stevenson III of Illinois. As chairman of a Senate subcommittee on migratory labor, Stevenson once made the following remarks for the record: "There was a time when we could campaign for public office, mount the step, and not fear a mortal wound from a tomato. If you're hit by a tomato today, you could suffer a grievous injury."

The senator, who grew up on a farm, prefers tomatoes that are plucked fresh from the garden. He made do without them during his student years at the Harvard Law School. Now he enjoys them occasionally when home on his family's new farm in Illinois. Actually, he doesn't mind hard tomatoes, as long as they're home-grown and fried in this fashion.

    2 large, green or underripe tomatoes, thickly sliced
    ½ cup flour (1 dL)
    1 tablespoon oregano
       salt and pepper to taste
    ½ cup bacon grease (1 dL)

Dredge the tomato slices in flour that has been seasoned with oregano, salt, and pepper. Heat the bacon grease in a skillet. Fry the tomatoes over medium heat for about 3 minutes per side, until they are slightly brown.

This recipe may be varied by flavoring the bacon grease with minced garlic or adding chopped fresh parsley to the seasoned flour. Fried tomatoes may be topped with a sprinkling of lemon juice.

Oil-Steeped Chinese Celery Cabbage

Serves 6

Cooking for crowds calls for confidence. Rulan Pian, professor of music and of East Asian languages and civilizations, gains her assurance from fail-safe dishes that can be cooked in a hurry. Pian enjoys serving supper to Harvard's homesick Chinese students and doesn't even mind their unannounced guests. She expands her banquets like a traditional Chinese chef, adding new dishes rather than enlarging the portions. Her cold, spicy cabbage makes a festive occasion even without a lot of company around. Serve it with her marinated chicken (page 148) and a real Chinese banquet is well under way.

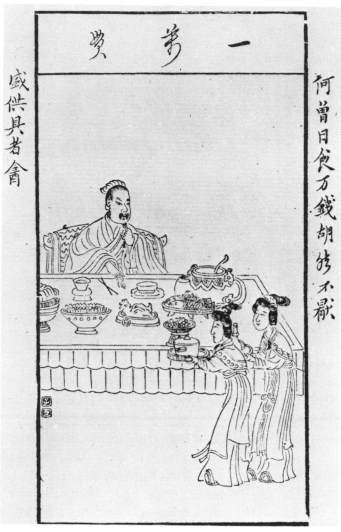

一 夢 雙

盛供具者膾

何曾日食万錢胡然不猒

Tseng Ho, a wealthy Chinese official of the third century, spent 10,000 coins daily seeking new culinary kicks. At this banquet, the concubines fail once again to please him, and Ho shows his anger by throwing down his chopsticks. The illustration is drawn from a seventeenth-century manuscript found among the rare treasures of the Harvard-Yenching Library.

2 Chinese celery cabbages, cut into 1½-inch rounds
5–6 cups boiling water (1¼–1½ L)
¼ cup corn oil (½ dL)
2 tablespoons sesame oil
1 teaspoon whole Szechwan peppercorns*
3 dried red peppers, whole
1 cup sugar (¼ L)
1 cup wine vinegar (¼ L)
1 tablespoon soy sauce

Arrange the cabbage rounds (intact, if possible) in a large dish that has a tight-fitting cover. Pour the boiling water over the cabbage to cover. Cover the dish and let it stand 15–20 minutes. Drain off the water.

Combine the corn and sesame oils in a small pan and place over high heat until the oils begin to crackle. Remove the pan from the heat. Add the peppercorns and whole red peppers and let the sauce stand for several minutes. Remove the red peppers and set them aside. Pour the sauce into the center of each cabbage round.

In a small bowl, combine the sugar, vinegar, and soy sauce, stirring until the sugar dissolves. Pour this mixture into the center of each cabbage round. Garnish the cabbage with the reserved red peppers. Cover and refrigerate until just before serving.

* These fragrant peppercorns, which are *not* hot, are available in Chinese markets. If the phrase "Szechwan peppercorns" doesn't ring a bell with the management, ask for *fa chew* (pronounced like a sneeze).

Fowl

[OVERLEAF] *A steel engraving from Charles Ranhofer's Franco-American cookbook,* The Epicurean, *at Radcliffe's Schlesinger Library. The volume features menus and recipes from Delmonico's in New York from 1862 to 1894, when Ranhofer was chef.*

Lime-Lemon Chicken Yassa

Serves 4

C hicken yassa is a West African dish with several variations, including the two listed here in succession. This Senegalese version, which weds chicken and citrus, is truly a memorable gustatory experience. Marcia Dambry discovered the stew while honeymooning in Dakar and recreated it when she got back to Cambridge. She also resumed work at the University Development office, where she documents the donation patterns of foundations and corporations. Dambry's reports are used by Harvard fund-raisers and by students and faculty members seeking support for their research. Here she documents the procedure for yassa according to her memory of the sharp, piquant flavor.

1½ cups lime and lemon juice, heavy on the lime
(3½ dL)*
3 tablespoons wine vinegar
4 onions, sliced
2 bay leaves
½ teaspoon salt
pepper to taste
1 2½–3-pound chicken, cut into serving pieces (1¼–
1½ kg)
1 tablespoon peanut oil

Combine the juices, vinegar, onions, and seasonings in a large bowl. Add the chicken pieces and stir to coat them with the marinade. If the marinade does not cover the chicken, add a little water (not more than ¾ cup, 1¾ dL). Cover and refrigerate for 6 hours or overnight.

Remove the chicken pieces, reserving the marinade with the onions. Broil the chicken for about 7 minutes per side, until brown. Heat the peanut oil in a large pot or heavy casserole. Add the onions and cook over medium heat until they begin to brown. Add the marinade and broiled chicken. Bring to a boil over high heat. Reduce the heat, cover, and simmer for about 30 minutes, until the meat is very tender. (If water was added to the marinade, remove the cover and simmer for another 5–10 minutes.)

Remove the bay leaves. Serve the yassa with boiled rice.

* This requires 6–10 fruits.

Spinach-Tomato Chicken Yassa

Serves 4

Eileen Southern, head of the Afro-American studies department at Harvard, remembers lime-lemon chicken yassa from her travels in West Africa, but prefers the version using spinach and tomatoes. Also a professor of music at Harvard, Southern has translated fifteenth-century song manuscripts into modern musical notation. Her translation of the yassa made in Senegal, Ghana, and the Ivory Coast tastes like the original dishes, she says, but her method of cooking the chicken adds "a strong dash of Afro-*American* flavor."

> 1 2½–3-pound chicken, cut into serving pieces (1¼–1½ kg)
> ½ teaspoon ginger
> 1 tablespoon salt
> 1 teaspoon white pepper
> 5 tablespoons peanut oil
> 1 large onion, finely chopped
> 4–5 cloves garlic, minced
> 3 celery stalks, finely chopped
> 3 tomatoes, finely chopped
> ½ cup tomato sauce (1 dL)
> 2 10-ounce packages fresh or frozen chopped spinach (57 dkg total)

Season the chicken with ginger, salt, and white pepper. Heat the oil in a large, deep skillet or pot. Add the chicken and cook over low heat 25–40 minutes, until it is cooked through. Remove the chicken and cover it to keep it warm.

Add to the skillet the onion, garlic, and celery, and cook until the onion turns clear. Add the tomatoes and tomato sauce, stirring to mix thoroughly. Add the spinach. If using fresh spinach, add it gradually, using a wooden spoon to press the leaves into the pan liquids. If using frozen spinach, defrost and drain it, then stir it into the onion-tomato mixture. Simmer for 20 minutes, stirring constantly. Thin the sauce with water if it becomes too thick.

Return the chicken to the skillet and simmer it in the sauce for another 2 minutes. Serve with boiled rice.

"Now sing we must." The emblem for the Krokodiloes, a male a cappella group at Harvard, features a beer-drinking crocodile in a hasty pudding pot. The drawing by "Krok" Alan Wachman (Class of 1980) suggests the historic liaison between the Krokodiloes and the Hasty Pudding Club.

Honey-Butter Chickens

Serves 12

=====

T he emblem for the Krokodiloes — a cheery crocodile brewing in a hasty pudding pot — documents
the early history of this male a cappella vocal
group. The "Kroks" got started in 1946, when four beer-
drinking members of the Hasty Pudding Club sang in
close harmony to entertain their friends. The team soon
added another three singers. When one of them suggested
that they name themselves the Krokodiloes (after the
Hasty Pudding librarian, who was Greek), a new singing
group was established at Harvard.

Today there are twelve voices in the Krokodiloes, including that of Alex Aldrich (Class of 1980). Aldrich, a
bass, enjoys the group's repertoire, which spans sixteenth-
century madrigals and Cole Porter tunes, and the itin-
erary, which includes bookings from New England to
Thailand.

Unlike his predecessors, Aldrich has never made or
tasted hasty pudding. He does, however, often dine with
his fellow Kroks. Occasionally Aldrich does the honors
himself. His two honeyed chickens can feed the full dozen.
For a smaller choir, the recipe is easily halved.

1 cup honey (¼ L)
2 sticks butter
2 tablespoons lemon juice
2 whole 3½–4-pound roasting chickens (1½–1¾ kg)
   salt and pepper to taste

In a saucepan, combine the honey, butter, and lemon
juice. Cook over low heat, stirring constantly, until
blended. Remove the saucepan from the heat.

Season the chickens with salt and pepper and place them in a large roasting pan. Brush them inside and out with half the honey-butter mixture. Bake at 350°F. (180°C) for about 1½ hours, basting with the pan juices every 10 minutes. Add a splash of the reserved honey-butter mixture several times during baking.

When the chickens are cooked through, place them on serving platters. Cover them to keep them warm. Skim the grease from the roasting pan. Add to the pan juices the remaining honey-butter mixture. Cook over high heat for several minutes, stirring constantly, until the sauce turns dark brown. Serve the sauce in a pitcher alongside the baked chickens.

Chicken with Basil

Serves 4

D avid Cohen, professor of education and social policy at the Graduate School of Education, loves to eat elaborate meals but doesn't like to cook them. He resolves the dilemma by banqueting in France for two weeks each fall. The rest of the year he's in Cambridge, perfecting simple specialties like this one.

   2 whole chicken breasts
   5 tablespoons butter
   ⅓ cup chopped fresh basil
     salt to taste

Split, skin, and bone the chicken. Crack the bones into small pieces and place them, with the skin, in a small pan. Add water to cover, and simmer for 45 minutes. Skim and strain the stock, return it to the pan, and simmer uncovered while preparing the chicken.

Melt 3 tablespoons of the butter in a skillet. Stir in the basil and salt. Add the chicken fillets and cook for 3 minutes per side until barely done. Remove the chicken and cover it to keep it warm. Melt the remaining butter in the skillet. Add the chicken stock and boil over high heat for several minutes, stirring until the mixture reduces slightly. Return the chicken breasts to the skillet, reduce the heat, and simmer for another minute. Serve with boiled rice.

Gabriel St. Aubin's eighteenth-century illustration of an "instructive" meal. (Courtesy of the Fogg Art Museum, Harvard University. Gift of Charles E. Dunlap.)

Foie de Volaille Prolétaire

Serves 2

"C hicken livers aren't expensive, which is part of their appeal," explains Doug Wornson, a factory worker and union organizer in South Boston. Wornson, a native Iowan, studied music at Harvard. He graduated in 1969 and headed for the assembly line, where he learned to make electrical components for tractors and trailers.

Wornson now also writes the newsletter for Local 262. To what use has he put his Harvard education? Wornson is expanding his foundation in music by studying classical and jazz guitar. And this recipe results indirectly from his years at Harvard. As a student, Wornson frequented various Harvard Square restaurants. One of his favorites offered modestly priced Brazilian food, including a chicken liver dish that resembles this one.

       2 tablespoons butter
       2 tablespoons vegetable oil
       ½ pound chicken livers (23 dkg)
       1 tablespoon flour
         salt and pepper to taste
         cayenne pepper to taste
       1 small onion, sliced
       1 large green pepper, cut into 1-inch pieces
       ⅓ cup inexpensive white wine (¾ dL)
       1 cup thinly sliced mushrooms (¼ L)

Heat the butter and oil in a skillet. Add the chicken livers and sprinkle with flour. Season with salt, pepper, and cayenne. Cook over medium high heat until the livers have browned and are nearly firm. Remove them with a slotted spoon. Cover them to keep them warm. Add to the skillet the onion, green pepper, and wine. Cook over medium heat until the onion turns clear. Add the mushrooms and cook until they turn soft. Return the livers to the skillet and cook for several minutes until they are firm. Serve plain or with boiled rice.

Chicken and Crab Meat Casserole

Serves 6

O ne way to escape from the congestion of Harvard Square is to take a scenic drive to Petersham, Massachusetts. There, no more than seventy miles west of Cambridge, the Harvard Forest offers 3000 acres for pleasant wooded walks as well as a museum illustrating the history of forestry.

The forest is also a center for instruction and research, and serves as the second home of Harvard biologist Ernest Gould. Gould is Harvard's "forest economist," which, in his words, means someone who promotes "high satisfaction forestry." He does this by determining how landowners can get what they want from their forest acres, be it scenic landscapes or a better harvest of wood. Gould's family recipe for chicken and crab meat is also designed to yield high satisfaction.

1 stick butter
2 tablespoons chopped onion
7 tablespoons flour
1 teaspoon salt
1 teaspoon paprika
1 teaspoon crushed rosemary
2 cups chicken broth (½ L)
2 cups sour cream (½ L)
3 cups cooked, diced chicken (¾ L)
1 cup cooked crab meat, drained (¼ L)
1½ cups cubed avocado (3½ dL)
1 tablespoon lemon juice
2 tablespoons butter, melted
1 cup dried bread crumbs (¼ L)

Melt the butter in a large, deep skillet. Add the onion and cook over low heat until it turns clear. Stir in the flour, salt, paprika, and rosemary. Cook for 4 minutes, stirring frequently. Add the chicken broth, stir, and remove the skillet from the heat. Gradually add the sour cream, stirring to blend thoroughly. Add the chicken and crab meat. Spoon the lemon juice over the cubed avocado. Stir this gently into the chicken–crab meat mixture. Pour the contents of the skillet into a 2-quart (2 L) baking dish.

Combine the melted butter with the bread crumbs. Sprinkle this on top of the casserole. Bake at 350°F. (180°C) for 30 minutes. Serve with boiled rice.

Lemon-Curry Chicken Kebabs

Serves 8–10

B F. Skinner has retired, but the pigeons are still around — in cages on the seventh floor of William James Hall. Five floors below lies the office of Dottie Lewis, business manager for all offices in this white high-rise building. Lewis's domain (referred to by students as "the ivory tower") is the department of psychology and social relations, where she supervises the entire budget, from pigeon feed to salaries.

Like Skinner, whose pigeons earned food for correct behaviors, Lewis believes in culinary rewards. She treats herself and dinner guests to a two-skewer menu. Here is her lemon-curried chicken with pineapple and green pepper — certainly as wonderful as the ingredients imply. To make the companion kabob, skewer beef, mushrooms, and onions; then marinate according to the recipe for Korean Fire Meat (p. 168).

½ cup lemon juice (1 dL)
¼ cup olive oil (½ dL)
1 tablespoon curry powder
1 tablespoon minced fresh ginger
1 teaspoon salt
¼ teaspoon cayenne pepper
3 pounds chicken breast fillets, cut into 1-inch pieces (1½ kg)
6 green peppers, cut into 1-inch pieces
4 cups pineapple cubes, drained (¾ L)

To make the marinade, combine the lemon juice, oil, and seasonings in a large bowl and stir to blend thoroughly. Add the chicken pieces and stir to coat them with the marinade. Cover and refrigerate for at least 3 hours, preferably overnight. Skewer the chicken alternately with the green peppers and pineapple. Cook over hot coals or under a broiler, basting with the marinade, until the chicken is cooked through.

Chicken with Ginger-Yogurt Sauce

Serves 6

Randee Brenner knew even less about cooking than she knew about Hebrew when she began working as a volunteer at Kibbutz Shoval, in Israel's Negev Desert. She became a kitchen trainee and soon learned to cook meals for four hundred people as well as to communicate, somewhat gingerly, in Hebrew.

Now a graduate student in Middle Eastern history at Harvard, Brenner conducts research in both Hebrew and Arabic. She also has a reputation as an excellent cook, especially among lovers of ginger, garlic, and lemon. Here those ingredients are used with chicken in a tangy yogurt sauce that is tinted yellow with spices. Once cooked, the sauce won't win any beauty contests, but the flavor will be exquisite.

1 32-ounce container plain yogurt (90 dkg)
⅓ cup lemon juice (¾ dL)
2 tablespoons minced fresh ginger
7 cloves garlic, pressed
1 tablespoon powdered saffron
1 teaspoon turmeric
½ teaspoon ground coriander
¼ teaspoon dry mustard
¼ teaspoon ground cardamom
  cayenne pepper to taste
3 whole chicken breasts, split and skinned

To make the marinade, combine all the ingredients except the chicken in a large bowl and stir to blend thoroughly. Add the chicken breasts and stir to coat them with the marinade. Cover and refrigerate overnight. Broil the chicken in the marinade for 15 minutes on each side or until the meat is cooked through. Serve with rice pilaf.

Shioji's Teriyaki

Serves 6

eri means "shiny" and _yaki_ means "broil," explains Hiroki Shioji, Harvard instructor in third-year Japanese. Shioji, who comes from Wakayama in southern Japan, has adapted teriyaki to suit his own tastes. His version calls for baking instead of broiling the meat, and removing the skin to cut down on calories.

Because many of his students have visited Japan, and because they have fairly advanced vocabularies, Shioji sometimes encourages culinary conversation. He introduces the subject by bringing teriyaki to class. There, as in Japan, one phrase begins the feasting. *Itadakimasu,* which means "received in humble appreciation," is the formal response that precedes digging in.

½ cup soy sauce (1 dL)
1–2 cups water (¼–½ L)
⅓ cup rice wine or other sweet white wine (¾ dL)*
1 tablespoon sugar
1 tablespoon minced fresh ginger
3 pounds chicken thighs and breasts, skinned (1½ kg)

To make the marinade, combine the liquid ingredients, sugar, and ginger in a large bowl. (For a stronger sauce, cut down on the water.) Add the chicken pieces and stir to coat them with the marinade. Cover and refrigerate for at least 3 hours.

Line a baking pan with aluminum foil, *teri* side down. Arrange the chicken pieces in the baking pan, adding marinade until it is ½-inch deep. Bake at 350°F (180°C) for 1 hour, turning the chicken every 10 minutes and basting with the marinade, until the chicken is cooked through. Serve hot with boiled rice or cold as a tailgate picnic before Harvard football games.

White-Cooked Chicken

Serves 4–6

Although Rulan Pian was born in Cambridge, she spent much of her childhood in mainland China. Her father (Class of 1918) taught Chinese and philosophy at Harvard and her mother has written several

---

* Rice wine, or *mirin,* can be purchased in Oriental markets and gourmet shops.

Chinese cookbooks, one of which Pian translated for publication in English. Pian claims that she's "not very filial," but she does maintain a close association with Harvard, and she is an excellent cook. A member of the Class of 1944, Pian received her Ph.D. in 1960. Now she is a member of the faculty, holding the University's only joint appointment in music and in East Asian studies. She also does plenty of good Chinese cooking, such as this cold marinated chicken and her oil-steeped cabbage (page 129). Both use a technique she did not learn from mother: cooking *off* the burner with boiling water.

7 quarts water (7 L)
1 2½–3-pound whole roasting chicken, at room temperature (1¼–1½ kg)
1 tablespoon sesame oil
2 tablespoons corn oil
¼ cup soy sauce (½ dL)
2 scallions, sliced

Bring the water to a full boil in an 8-quart (8 L) pot with a tight-fitting lid. Remove the pot from the heat and add the whole chicken. Cover and let stand for at least 2 hours. Remove the chicken from the water and let it cool. The meat should be cooked through and very tender. Pull the meat from the bones and place in a serving bowl.

Combine the two oils in a small pan over medium heat. When the oil begins to crackle, remove the pan from the heat and stir in the soy sauce. Add the scallions, stir, and pour the sauce over the chicken. Cover and refrigerate until just before serving.

Pian notes that this cooking technique also works well with fish: Place fillets in a dish and cover them with boiling water. Let them stand, covered, for 10–20 minutes until the fish is just beginning to flake. Pour on the same marinade. Cover and refrigerate until just before serving.

(149)

From a rare first edition of one of the earliest illustrated cookbooks comes this elaborate woodcut of a nobleman's kitchen. Banchetti compositioni di vivande, *published in 1549, was written by Christoforo di Messi Spughi, kitchen superintendent to the Duke of Ferrara. The book contains the menus, guest lists, and recipes used for banquets he catered while employed by the Duke. (By permission of the Houghton Library, Harvard University.)*

Canard aux Pommes

(Duck with Apples)

Serves 2

━━━━━━━━━━━━━━━━━━━━━━━━━━━━━━━━━━━━━━

For classic French food in an elegant atmosphere, Maison Robert is one of the best restaurants in Boston. The establishment, owned by Ann Robert (A.M. 1956) and her husband, Lucien, occupies what was once the treasurer's office in Boston's Old City Hall. The décor includes many of the original chandeliers and mirrors, reflecting the style of the French Second Empire. The cuisine reflects Lucien Robert's Norman background, often featuring the apples and apple liqueur characteristic of regional cooking in Normandy.

In their own house, as in the Maison Robert, this Norman tradition is celebrated in style. Ann Robert learned how to prepare this duck from her French sister-in-law. The recipe calls for *canard* in a brown sauce of cider, cream, and liqueur, garnished with golden cooked slices of *pomme*.

  1 3½–4-pound duck, cleaned (1½–1¾ kg)
    salt and pepper
  ¼ cup clarified butter (½ dL)
  6–8 Golden Delicious apples, peeled, cored, and quartered
  ¾ cup dry apple cider or dry white wine (1¾ dL)
  ½ cup apple liqueur or blended apple whiskey (1 dL)
  ½ cup heavy cream (1 dL)
  1 tablespoon butter

Season the duck with salt and pepper, and truss it. Place it in a roasting pan on top of the stove and brown it quickly on all sides over high heat. Roast the duck at 400°F

(205°C) until the juices that run from the joints are clear, about 40–50 minutes.

Meanwhile, cook the apples on both sides in the clarified butter until they are golden. Remove them with a slotted spoon and keep them warm.

When the duck is cooked through, place it on a heated serving platter. Cover it to keep it warm. Skim off the grease in the roasting pan and deglaze the remaining pan liquids with the cider or wine. Reduce this liquid over high heat to half its original volume. Pour on the liqueur or whiskey and flame off the alcohol. Reduce the heat. Add the heavy cream and the tablespoon of butter, stirring to blend thoroughly. Remove the sauce from the heat and cover it.

Carve the duck into serving pieces. Arrange the apple slices around the duck. Spoon the sauce on top.

Rock Cornish Hens with Herb-Walnut Stuffing

Serves 4

Jim Shapiro (Class of 1968) actually runs 100 miles at one time, a journey that takes more than 16 hours. Before an ultra-marathon, Shapiro loads up on carbohydrates. During the race, he pauses at intervals to drink fruit juice mixtures. After crossing the finish line, he is ready to feast. These Rock Cornish hens, perfectly roasted and stuffed, are one of the meals he enjoys coming home to.

4 1-pound Rock Cornish hens (46-dkg each)
  salt and pepper
5 tablespoons sweet butter
½ pint heavy cream (¼ L)
1 teaspoon rosemary
1 teaspoon thyme
1 teaspoon basil
1 teaspoon dill
1½ tablespoons chopped fresh parsley
  pinch nutmeg
  salt and pepper to taste
2 cups cubed French or Italian bread (½ L)
¼ cup finely chopped boiled ham (½ dL)
½ cup chopped walnuts (1 dL)
½ cup white wine (1 dL)
½ cup chicken broth (1 dL)

Trim off the wing tips and season each hen with salt and pepper. Place a dab of butter in each cavity, reserving half the butter.

To make the stuffing, combine the cream, seasonings, bread, ham, and walnuts in a large bowl, stirring to mix thoroughly. Stuff the hens with the mixture and place them in a deep roasting pan, breast side up. (Shapiro doesn't bother to truss the hens.) Dot the breasts with the remaining butter. Pour the wine and chicken broth into the pan. Bake 40–50 minutes, basting occasionally, until the skin is golden brown and the meat is cooked through.

To complete the meal, Shapiro serves a salad and steamed broccoli with butter and lime juice.

Beef and Veal

Steak and Kidney Pie
with Oysters

Serves 6

T he Nieman Program, which provides journalists with a nine-month study sabbatical at Harvard, was implemented in 1937 by Harvard President James B. Conant. The program was established through a gift from Agnes Wahl Nieman "to promote and elevate" American journalism, and to honor the memory of her husband, Lucius, founder of the Pulitzer Prize–winning *Milwaukee Journal.*

Each year since its founding, between twelve and twenty Nieman fellows (from this country and elsewhere) have availed themselves of the full range of Harvard opportunities. Like hungry guests at an elaborate smorgasbord, they sample courses, graduate seminars, and special study groups. Canadian radio producer Mike Mc-Ivor, a Nieman fellow in 1978, entered the experience with traditional gusto, studying history, economics, and the writings of Samuel Johnson.

McIvor's contribution to the Harvard buffet is this meat pie with oysters, which he learned to prepare during one of many trips to England. McIvor likes to call attention to his culinary credentials: he once spent five months as cook on a salmon packer in the Pacific.

¾ pound beef kidneys (34 dkg)
1 pound round steak, trimmed of fat and cut into
    1-inch pieces (46 dkg)
¼ cup flour (½ dL)
3 tablespoons liquid gravy enhancer
2 teaspoons Worcestershire sauce
    salt and pepper to taste
    cayenne pepper to taste
1 small onion, finely chopped
¼ cup chopped fresh parsley (½ dL)
½ pint shucked oysters, drained (¼ L)
    pastry for a 9-inch double-crust pie
    butter

Soak the beef kidneys in water for 2 hours. Separate the sections and trim off the gristle. Place the kidney pieces and steak in a large pot and just cover with water. Simmer uncovered for 2 hours.

Remove the meat with a slotted spoon and set it aside. Gradually add the flour to the beef stock, stirring over low heat until the gravy thickens. Add the gravy enhancer, Worcestershire sauce, salt, pepper, cayenne, onion, and parsley. Remove the pot from the heat.

Line the pie plate with the bottom crust. Combine the drained oysters with the steak and kidneys, and spoon this mixture into the unbaked pie shell. Pour about ¼ of the gravy over this filling. Arrange the top crust over the pie, trimming and crimping the edges to form a sealed border. Make 4–5 slits in the top crust. Bake at 400°F (205°C) for 30 minutes. Reduce the temperature to 200°F (95°C) and continue baking for 25 minutes. Dot the top with butter and bake for another five minutes.

McIvor serves the pie with mashed potatoes and generously spoons the gravy over both.

"Eat right and avoid the plague" is the general message behind this woodcut, published in The Book of Pestilence (Das Buch der Pestilentz) *in Strassburg in 1500. The guide to good health and hygiene by Hieronymus Brunschwig is preserved in Harvard's Francis A. Countway Library of Medicine.*

Beef Stroganoff

Serves 4

Massachusetts Senator Edward M. Kennedy (Class of 1954) comes from a family long associated with Harvard. That association was commemorated in 1978 with the dedication of Harvard's John Fitzgerald Kennedy School of Government. The school's program is designed to provide professional training for those pursuing careers in public service.

Kennedy's own career as a public servant has been well recorded. But one little-known fact about the senator is that he is an excellent cook. One of his specialties is this perfect beef stroganoff, which has become another family tradition.

6	tablespoons butter
1	tablespoon flour
1	cup beef broth (¼ L)
	ginger to taste
½	pound sliced fresh mushrooms (23 dkg)
1	onion, finely chopped
2	pounds beef tenderloin, trimmed of fat and cut into finger-sized strips (90 dkg)
	salt and pepper
1½	cups sour cream (3½ dL)

Melt 2 tablespoons of the butter in a skillet. Add the flour, stirring and cooking for several minutes until slightly brown. Gradually add the beef broth, stirring constantly. Bring the mixture to a boil and whisk until it thickens. Add ginger. Place the mixture in a pot or Dutch oven (off the stove). Cover to keep it warm.

Melt 2 tablespoons of the remaining butter in the skillet. Add the mushrooms and cook until they turn soft, then add them to the pot. Melt the remaining butter in the skillet. Add the chopped onion and cook until it turns golden. Season the beef strips with salt and pepper, and add them to the onions. Cook the meat quickly over high heat. Add the contents of the skillet to the pot.

Place the pot on the stove over low heat. Gradually stir in the sour cream. Cook for several minutes until the sour cream is warm and thoroughly blended.

Senator Kennedy serves the stroganoff with rice or noodles, and buttered spinach that has been seasoned with nutmeg.

Cornish Pasties

Makes 10 individual pasties or 1 9-inch pie

The Signet Society is one of Harvard's century-old institutions. Founded in 1870 as a club for Harvard juniors, the Signet sought members with "marked literary ability" — and, indeed, among the names on the membership roster, one finds such luminaries as T. S. Eliot and Samuel Eliot Morison. New members are expected to show the same promise and must give an oration as part of their initiation.

The Signet Society chef is part of a literary family herself, a fact that is documented in her book *My Father, Bertrand Russell.* Kate Tait (Class of 1944, Ph.D. '71) is in charge of the society's weekday lunches and annual dinners.

Tait's British background is reflected in her cooking. She first encountered pasties during summer visits to

Good King Wenceslas exhibits his saintly generosity in a book of that title illustrated by Arthur J. Gaskin. It was published in Birmingham in 1895. (By permission of the Houghton Library, Harvard University.)

Cornwall, where they made good portable lunches for farmers and miners, and good sixpenny snacks for growing girls. Pasties are now found on the Signet House table — as individual crescents or whole meat pies.

THE PASTRY

½ cup boiling water (1 dL)
1 cup lard at room temperature (¼ L)
3 cups sifted flour (¾ L)
1 teaspoon baking powder
1 teaspoon salt

THE FILLING

½ pound ground beef (23 dkg)
1 onion, chopped
1 potato, diced
¼ cup diced turnip (½ dL)
1 teaspoon salt
¼ teaspoon pepper
thyme to taste
2 tablespoons chopped fresh parsley
Worcestershire sauce to taste

1 egg, beaten

To make the pastry, pour the boiling water over the lard and beat until the lard is cool and creamy. Sift the dry ingredients together and combine them with the lard mixture to form a smooth dough. Shape the dough into a ball, handling as little as possible. Wrap it in plastic wrap and refrigerate until it is firm.

For the filling, combine the rest of the ingredients except for the egg and mix thoroughly.

Roll out the dough on a floured surface. To form individual pasties, cut the dough into 6- or 7-inch circles. Place some filling on each circle and moisten the edge with water or a bit of the beaten egg. Fold in half to form

(163)

a crescent and crimp the edges with the prongs of a fork. Make two small slits on top of each pasty and place on a lightly greased baking sheet. Brush the tops with the beaten egg. Bake at 425°F (220°C) for 30–40 minutes.

To make a meat pie, use half the dough to line a 9-inch pie plate. Add the filling and cover with the remaining dough. Trim and crimp the edges to form a sealed border. Make four or five slits in the top of the pie and brush with the beaten egg. Bake at 425°F (220°C) for about 50 minutes.

Low-Sodium Swiss Steak

Serves 4

Nutritionist Martha Singer offers a cooking class for cardiology patients at Harvard's School of Public Health. Singer shows her students palatable ways to avoid fat, cholesterol, and salt. Her low-sodium Swiss steak meets all the requirements, using lean beef, polyunsaturated oil, and salt-free seasonings.

The first version of Singer's recipe contains about 460 milligrams of sodium per serving, with a mere 100 milligrams per serving in the strict low-sodium adaptation that follows. Both have a healthy dose of real Swiss steak flavor.

1½ pounds lean round steak (68 dkg)
½ cup flour (1 dL)
¼ teaspoon pepper
¼ cup polyunsaturated cooking oil (½ dL)
1 large onion, sliced
1 1-pound can tomatoes (46 dkg)
1 8-ounce can tomato sauce (23 dkg)
¼ teaspoon garlic powder
⅛ teaspoon celery seed
1 bay leaf
2 tablespoons chopped fresh parsley

Trim the steak of fat and cut into four 3-by-5-inch pieces. If the steak is more than ¾ inch thick, slice each piece in half to reduce the thickness. Dredge the meat in flour that has been seasoned with pepper. Place the meat on a cutting board. Using a mallet or the edge of a heavy plate, pound the flour into the meat, coating with more flour as needed, until the pieces are ¼–½ inch thick.

Heat 1 tablespoon of the oil in a large skillet. Add the onion and cook over medium heat until it turns clear. Brown the meat in the same skillet, adding oil as needed. Remove the steak and onions from the skillet and set them aside. Combine the remaining ingredients in the skillet and stir to mix thoroughly. Return the onion and meat to the skillet and spoon the sauce on top. Cover the skillet and simmer until the meat is tender, about 1 hour.

To accommodate those on a strict low-sodium diet, use low-sodium canned tomatoes or 1 pound (46 dkg) fresh tomatoes, peeled and chopped. Instead of tomato sauce, use low-sodium tomato juice or ½ pound (23 dkg) fresh tomatoes, puréed.

To complete the meal, Singer recommends steamed broccoli and salad with noodles, whole grain rice, or enriched white rice.

Ragout of Beef with Blanched Orange Rind

Serves 4

The Harvard Business School was founded in 1908, based on the notion "that administration of business enterprises needed to be and could be a professional matter, worthy of the time and attention of learned, thoughtful, and responsible men and women."

Edna Hunt, from Haifa, Israel, agrees. In 1954 she became the first woman to apply to the school for admission. Hunt was admitted, earned a doctorate in business administration, and now serves as a business consultant for hospitals and other enterprises in the Boston area.

"Learned, thoughtful, and responsible" not only as a consultant but also as a cook, Hunt is known locally as a true epicure. Her reputation is confirmed by this beef ragout, a robust dish delicately flavored with orange.

> 3 tablespoons bacon fat
> 2 pounds top round steak, trimmed of fat and cut into
>   1½-inch pieces (90 dkg)
> 1 onion, finely chopped
> 1–2 cloves garlic, crushed
> 1 tablespoon flour
> ½ cup red wine (1 dL)
> 2 cups beef stock or undiluted consommé (½ L)
>   salt and pepper to taste

Bouquet garni:

- 3 parsley sprigs
- 1 bay leaf
- 6 whole peppercorns
- ½ teaspoon thyme
- ½ teaspoon basil

- 1 orange
- 2 tablespoons sweet butter
- 5 celery hearts, trimmed of leaves, shaved, and cut into 1½-inch pieces
- ½ cup walnut halves (1 dL)

Heat the bacon fat in a large pot or heavy casserole. Add the meat and brown it, in batches if necessary. Remove the meat with a slotted spoon and set it aside. Add the onion and garlic and cook over low heat until the onion begins to brown. Stir in the flour and cook for several minutes. Add the wine and return the meat to the pot. Add enough beef stock or consommé to not quite cover the meat. Season with salt and pepper and the bouquet garni (spices and seasonings wrapped in cheesecloth and tied with white string). Bring to a boil. Reduce the heat, cover, and simmer for at least 1½ hours, stirring occasionally, until the meat is tender. (This much can be done ahead of time. Cover, refrigerate, and skim off surface fats when ready to proceed.)

Peel the orange and squeeze several sections to make 2 tablespoons orange juice. Set the juice aside. Cut the orange peel into very fine strips. Blanch these for 5 minutes in boiling water. Drain and refresh by placing them in cold water.

Meanwhile, melt the butter in a skillet. Add the celery and cook over medium heat for 5 minutes. Add the walnuts and cook for 1–2 minutes. Add the celery and walnuts to the ragout along with the 2 tablespoons orange juice.

Drain the orange rind and remove the bouquet garni from the pot. Garnish the ragout with the blanched orange rind.

Hunt serves buttered noodles and green beans with this dish.

Bul-Kogi
(Korean Fire Meat)

Serves 4

T his culinary composition comes from Earl Kim, the James Edward Ditson Professor of Music. Kim likes the dish because it always pleases his guests, and because it is so easy to prepare.

"Fire meat," Kim notes, refers to the cooking method, not the spiciness. He learned from his North Korean mother and South Korean father that authentic bul-kogi is cooked over charcoal and served with rice. Kim adds the touch of a native Californian. He cooks his fire meat over a burner, then serves it with rice and a tossed salad.

2–2½ pounds flank steak (¾–1¼ kg)
  ¼ cup soy sauce (½ dL)
  1 tablespoon sesame oil
  1 scallion, minced
  1 clove garlic, minced
  2 teaspoons minced fresh ginger
     pinch of sugar
  1 tablespoon white sesame seeds, toasted and crushed

Trim the meat of fat and cut it into slices about 2 inches long and ⅛ inch thick.

Combine the remaining ingredients in a large bowl to make the marinade, and stir to blend thoroughly. Add the meat and stir to coat each piece with the marinade. Cover and refrigerate for 15–30 minutes. (Kim notes that beef tends to toughen if it marinates in soy sauce for more than a half hour.)

Place a wok or heavy skillet over high heat until it begins to smoke. Add the meat and the marinade and stir-fry for no more than 3–4 minutes. Kim's technique is to stir the meat for a minute, let it rest for a minute, stir again, and so on.

Keep Kim's marinade in mind during barbeque season. Beef cubes marinated in the mixture for 30 minutes are excellent in shish kebabs that include onions and mushrooms (see page 145).

Texas Chili

Serves 10

Real Texas chili has just five ingredients: meat, chili peppers, cumin seeds, salt, and water. Even though they are native Texans, or perhaps because they are, Joe and Faye Wyatt take liberties with the recipe, which they cook up to serve eighty guests.

Chili parties remind the Wyatts of the flavors of home, but Cambridge has provided new experiences to savor. Joe is the vice president for administration at Harvard, as well as a senior lecturer on computer science. Faye is active in Harvard Neighbors, a service group that welcomes newcomers to the University. Together the Wyatts have taught New England friends to make chili, and learned from them how to make New England chowder.

1½ ounces beef suet, chopped (45 g)
4½ pounds beef chuck, cut into ½-inch pieces (2 kg)
2 onions, finely chopped
2 cloves garlic, minced
1½ teaspoons salt
5 tablespoons chili powder
1–5 dried red peppers, finely chopped
1½ teaspoons ground cumin
1½ pounds pinto beans, cooked, and their liquid
(68 dkg)

Cook the suet in a large cast iron pot until its fat is rendered. Discard the remaining suet bits, or follow the Wyatt's suggestion and feed them to the bird dog. Brown the meat over high heat. Reduce the heat, add the onions and garlic, and simmer 20–30 minutes, until the meat begins to dry out.

Add the salt, chili powder, red peppers, cumin, and water to cover. Simmer for at least 2½ hours, stirring frequently. Skim off the surface fat. (At this point you can refrigerate the chili overnight. It will get hotter as it matures. The next day skim off the surface fat before proceeding.)

Drain the cooked pinto beans (reserving their liquid) and mash them. Add the mashed beans to the simmering chili mixture and stir to mix thoroughly. Stir in enough bean liquid to thin and flavor the chili to taste. Simmer the beans and chili 15–20 minutes, stirring occasionally.

Serve in large bowls with crackers, tortillas, or *jalapeño* cornbread. The Wyatts provide salad, beer, iced tea, and water to cool their guests' palates.

Ground Beef with Herbs

Serves 1

If French is a language of words and of gestures, then Professor Laurence Wylie is totally fluent. Wylie, the C. Douglas Dillon Professor of the Civilization of France, spent his sabbatical from Harvard in Paris as a student of mime. Now those enrolled in his class "Communicating with the French" are expected to master the exquisite shades of meaning in the Gallic shrug, as well as the proper use of the past participle.

Wylie knows how to gesture when a cab driver nearly runs him down, when a speaker tells a boring story, and when a meal is finely made. After the first mouthful of this ground beef entrée — which he learned from his wife, Anne — Wylie responds with a classic gesture. "*Splendide!*" is the message his thrown kiss conveys. It shows Wylie's appreciation for beef, mushrooms, and herbs.

¼–½ pound lean ground beef (12–23 dkg)
1 slice whole wheat bread
1 tablespoon butter
1 tablespoon prepared horseradish
basil or tarragon to taste
salt and pepper to taste
5 mushroom caps

Make a nest of ground beef on the slice of whole wheat bread. Place the butter and horseradish inside the hollow. Sprinkle the basil or tarragon (fresh or dried) on top. Add salt and pepper. Cover with mushroom caps and season again. Wylie places this creation on a piece of aluminum foil with the edges turned up, to avoid dirtying any dishes. He bakes it at 400°F (205°C) for a mere 20 minutes, until the surface of the meat is crusty and the inside is rare.

Cuban Beef Picadillo

Serves 4

When the Dominguez family left Cuba for the United States in 1960, they bid farewell to their household chef. After they resettled, Señora Dominguez, then in her late thirties, made her first (often disastrous) efforts at cooking. Jorge Dominguez, then a teenager, learned from Mother's mistakes.

Now an associate professor of government at Harvard, Dominguez teaches courses on Latin American politics. He has chronicled the events leading to and following his family's emigration in *Cuba: Order and Revolution*, published by Harvard University Press.

Meanwhile, he has learned some cooking tricks on his own. Dominguez has simplified ("for technological convenience") this traditional Cuban beef dish. In Cuba, picadillo might include hot peppers and vegetables. Here, too, the recipe can accommodate additions, from hot sauce to the liquid in bottled green olives.

    1 pound ground beef (46 dkg)
    1 small green pepper, finely chopped
    1 onion, finely chopped
    4 cloves garlic, minced
    ½ teaspoon salt
    6 pimiento-stuffed green olives, sliced
    2 tablespoons red wine
    1 8-ounce can tomato sauce (23 dkg)

Combine all the ingredients in a skillet and cook over high heat for 5 minutes, stirring frequently. Reduce the heat and simmer for 30 minutes. Dominguez serves the picadillo as they do in Cuba — on a bed of boiled rice and topped with fried eggs.

Dear Ann's Meat Loaf

Serves 6

A nn Landers is well known for her domestic advice, a lot of which does not relate to the kitchen. In addition to being the most widely syndicated columnist in the world, she was named by United Press International as one of the most influential women in the country.

Landers's genuine concern for her readers' health and tranquillity is evident beyond her column in 960 American newspapers. Among her additional activities, she is an enthusiastic member of the visiting committee at the Harvard Medical School. This group, like all of Harvard's sixty-odd visiting committees, is made up of interested and knowledgeable people (usually *not* members of the faculty or staff) who report to the Board of Overseers on developments in their designated schools or departments. For Landers, this means meeting with the medical faculty, staff, and students, who keep her informed on current medical research.

At committee meetings in Cambridge, as elsewhere in her private life, Ann Landers goes by another name. This piece of advice on making Midwestern meat loaf comes direct from Eppie Lederer of Sioux City, Iowa.

2 pounds ground round steak (90 dkg)
2 eggs, lightly beaten
1½ cups dried bread crumbs (3½ dL)
¾ cup ketchup (1¾ dL)
1 teaspoon monosodium glutamate
½ cup warm water (1 dL)
1 1½-ounce package dried onion soup mix (40 g)
2 bacon strips
1 8-ounce can tomato sauce (23 dkg)

In a large bowl, combine the beef, eggs, bread crumbs, ketchup, monosodium glutamate, water, and onion soup mix. Stir to mix thoroughly. Place the mixture in a 5-by-9-inch loaf pan. Arrange the bacon strips on top and cover with the tomato sauce. Bake at 350°F (180°C) for 1 hour.

Lemon-Veal Ragout

Serves 8

Gerry Pierce earned his master's degree from the Harvard Divinity School in 1968, but soon he responded to another calling. In 1970 he established the Peasant Stock Restaurant on Washington Street, several blocks from Harvard Yard. After building the kitchen and modeling a cozy dining room, Pierce organized a staff of Harvard students. Opening night the team served this veal ragout, which was so well received it became a house specialty.

The restaurant has since grown in size and reputation. The menu, which changes nightly, still features hearty Mediterranean cuisine, with a reliable selection of good soups and stews, and an impressive wine list with fifty-five entries.

The clientele of the restaurant, for some unknown reason, includes an inordinate number of lovelorn couples who fall apart or come together over Peasant Stock dinners. "We've had more than our share of teary-eyed customers," says Pierce. "Our waiters and waitresses have learned to be sensitive." Other customers include Divinity School professors, Massachusetts politicians, and local musicians. The musicians perform a wide range of classical and folk music in the restaurant's newly redecorated back room. Their payment is made in the form of a barter — an appreciative audience and a hearty meal.

1½ tablespoons butter
1½ tablespoons vegetable oil
4 bacon strips, cut into 1½-inch pieces
4 pounds stewing veal, trimmed of fat and cut into 1-inch pieces
¾ teaspoon marjoram
¼ teaspoon cayenne pepper
1 tablespoon salt
3 tablespoons flour
2 cups chicken stock (½ L)
1 cup dry white wine or vermouth (¼ L)
2 bay leaves
1 tablespoon Worcestershire sauce
1 lemon, sliced into 8 rounds
1 10-ounce package frozen artichoke hearts (29 dkg)
½ cup heavy cream (1 dL)
sliced lemon rounds and chopped fresh dill for garnish

Melt the butter in a heavy casserole or Dutch oven. Add the oil, bacon, and veal. Cook over low heat for several minutes until the veal is lightly browned. Add the marjoram, cayenne, and salt. Sprinkle with the flour, stir, and cook for 2–3 minutes. Add the chicken stock, wine, bay leaves, and Worcestershire sauce. Stir to mix thoroughly. Arrange the lemon slices on top. Cover and simmer (or cover and place in a 350°F (180°C) oven) for 1–1½ hours, until the veal is tender.

Discard the lemon slices. Add the artichoke hearts and simmer uncovered for 5–7 minutes, until they are tender. Remove the bay leaves and stir in the heavy cream. Garnish with a fresh batch of thinly sliced lemon rounds and the chopped dill.

Peasant Stock chefs serve this ragout with buttered noodles and a fresh red or green vegetable.

From the Dictionnaire de l'académie des gastronomes, *housed in Radcliffe's Schlesinger Library.*

Veal Marengo

Serves 4

Supposedly invented by Napoleon's chef to honor the emperor's Austrian conquest, marengo has a special place in culinary history. The contributor of this recipe knows that history well. Over the course of some fifty years, Narcissa Chamberlain and her husband, Samuel, collected more than a thousand gastronomical volumes. The books, a gift to Radcliffe's Schlesinger Library, comprise an outstanding selection of regional French cookbooks from the eighteenth century on. The collection also includes culinary treatises from Italy, Britain, and the United States, as well as cookbooks published and illustrated by the Chamberlains themselves.

Choosing one recipe from this culinary empire presented quite a challenge to Narcissa Chamberlain. In the end, the honor went to "Veau Sauté Marengo" from *The Flavor of France*. The authors? Narcissa and her daughter, Narcisse, with photographs by Samuel Chamberlain.*

4–5 tablespoons butter
12 mushroom caps
12 tiny whole onions
3 tablespoons olive oil
1½ pounds tender stewing veal, trimmed of fat and cut into 1½-inch pieces (68 dkg)
4 peeled, seeded, and finely chopped tomatoes
2 teaspoons flour
1 cup dry white wine (¼ L)
2 cups chicken stock or undiluted consommé (½ L)
1 clove garlic
salt and pepper to taste

* © Copyright 1960, by permission of Hastings House, Publishers.

(177)

Melt 2 tablespoons of the butter in a skillet. Add the mushrooms and cook 3–4 minutes. Remove the mushrooms with a slotted spoon and set them aside. Melt the remaining butter in the skillet. Add the onions and cook over medium heat until they begin to brown. Remove them with a slotted spoon and set them aside.

Heat the olive oil in a heavy casserole. Add the veal and brown quickly over high heat. Reduce the heat, add the tomatoes, and return the onions to the casserole. Simmer 4–5 minutes. Sprinkle with flour and stir to blend thoroughly. Add the wine, chicken stock, garlic, salt, and pepper. Cover and simmer for 1 hour, stirring occasionally. Add the mushroom caps and simmer uncovered for another 30 minutes, until the veal is tender. Garnish with chopped parsley and serve with croutons. Buttered noodles and salad go nicely with marengo.

Continental Veal Roll

Serves 8–10

I'm not sure if my interest in chemistry fostered an interest in cooking — or if it happened the other way around," says Margaret Ball, who graduated in 1938. Ball, now a Harvard associate in surgery, conducts metabolic research at Peter Bent Brigham, one of thirteen Harvard teaching hospitals in the Boston area.

Ball also enjoys metabolic research of a more epicurean nature. She has taken cooking lessons in Paris and London and now teaches continental cookery for Harvard Neighbors. Her lessons include this plan for rolled and stuffed veal, an elegant repast served hot or cold.

1 6–6½ pound breast of veal with bones (2¾–3 kg)
1 cup sausage meat, removed from the casing (¼ L)
¾ pound lean ground beef (34 dkg)
½ cup dried bread crumbs (1 dL)
1 egg, lightly beaten
1 clove garlic, minced
¼ teaspoon thyme
½ teaspoon rosemary
¼ cup sherry (½ dL)
  salt and pepper
1 tablespoon mixed marjoram, thyme, and rosemary
1 onion, sliced
1 celery stalk with leaves, cut into several pieces
1 carrot, sliced
  veal stock or water

Bone the veal, reserving all bones (or ask your butcher to bone it and give you the bones). In a large bowl, combine the sausage meat, ground beef, bread crumbs, egg, garlic, ¼ teaspoon thyme, ½ teaspoon rosemary, and sherry. Mix thoroughly. Lay the veal on a flat work surface. Season it with salt and pepper, and rub with the 1 tablespoon mixed herbs. Using a spoon or spatula, spread the sausage mixture on the veal, leaving a 2-inch margin on all sides. Roll the veal like a jelly roll and secure it by tying with white string in several places. Wrap the rolled loaf in cheesecloth and knot the ends.

Place the veal bones in a large pot or heavy casserole. Lay the veal roll on top. Add the onion, celery, and carrot. Add the veal stock or water to cover. Cover and simmer for 2 hours. Remove the veal roll from the pot and discard the cheesecloth, leaving the strings intact. Place in a pan and lay a plate or board on top. Arrange 5 pounds of weight (2¼ kg) on this support in order to flatten and press the loaf. (Ball uses lead containers used for mailing isotopes from her lab.) Refrigerate overnight.

Reduce the liquids in which the veal was cooked to

about 2 cups (½ L). Strain the stock. Remove the white strings from the veal roll and slice. To serve hot, heat the stock and thicken, if necessary, with flour or potato starch. Arrange the sliced veal in a large baking dish and spoon the sauce on top. Heat in a 300°F (150°C) oven for 30 minutes. Ball serves the veal roll with boiled carrots or spinach, and rice pilaf.

To convert the dish into a cold veal galantine, clarify the stock. Dissolve 2 tablespoons unflavored gelatin in the heated stock and let it cool. Place the veal slices on a rack over waxed paper. Spoon on a layer of gelatin and allow the glaze to stiffen. Then decorate the surface with flowers made from carrot slices. Carefully spoon on another layer of glaze. Refrigerate until just before serving.

Veal Lafayette

Serves 6

Ed Sullivan knows advertising from a number of angles. As director of advertising at *Harvard Magazine*, he's experienced in selling and laying out ads. Also a model who is featured *in* ads, he dons jogging outfits in *Sports Illustrated*, business suits in *Women's Wear Daily*, and "a wife and a suitcase" in Howard Johnson's brochures.

Sullivan is also an accomplished cook, but his dual careers leave little time for the hobby. This well-designed veal dish — topped with sliced tomato and avocado — suits him because it is quickly prepared.

6 veal scallops, ⅛-inch thick
½ cup flour (1 dL)
2 cloves garlic, minced
1 tablespoon paprika
   salt and pepper
3 tablespoons butter
3 tablespoons olive oil
1 tablespoon minced shallots or scallions
⅛ teaspoon sage
¾ cup veal or chicken stock (1¾ dL)
⅓ cup port or other sweet wine (¾ dL)
2-3 tomatoes, thinly sliced
1 ripe avocado, peeled and sliced
1 cup grated Parmesan or Gruyère (¼ L)

Heat a deep serving platter. Dredge the veal scallops in flour that has been seasoned with garlic, paprika, salt, and pepper. Heat the butter and olive oil in a large skillet. Add the veal and cook briefly over high heat on both sides until light brown. Place the veal on the heated serving platter. Cover the platter and keep it warm.

Cook the shallots with the sage in the skillet until the shallots turn golden. Add the stock and wine. Reduce over high heat to half the original volume.

Meanwhile, arrange slices of tomato and avocado on each veal scallop. Dust with half the grated cheese. Preheat the broiler and spoon the sauce over the veal. Top with the remaining cheese. Place under the broiler 1-2 minutes, until the cheese is melted.

Lamb, Pork, and Other Meats

[OVERLEAF] *Title page* of Culina Famulatrix Medicinae: or Receipts in Cookery. *This early nineteenth-century volume by A. Hunter claims to be "worthy of the notice of those medical practitioners, who ride in their chariots with a footman behind, and who receive two-guinea fees from their rich and luxurious patients." The book is housed at Radcliffe's Schlesinger Library.*

Lamb Transmontana

Serves 8–10

T̶he food of Trás-os-Montes ("behind the moun-
tains") deserves better press, according to assistant
professor Noel Ortega. This province of northern
Portugal is known to Europeans for its witches and their
herbed rabbit stew. In Portuguese literature — Ortega's
specialty — it is the least touted province when it comes
to cuisine.

Ortega has been trying to rectify the situation. After
earning his B.A. at Harvard's Extension School in 1969,
he carried the word through the Faculty of Arts and Sciences (Ph.D. 1974).

Now as an assistant professor of Romance languages
and literature at Harvard, Ortega devotes one class each
year to Transmontana cooking. He holds the session in a
South House kitchen, where students read recipes and

cook in Portuguese. One favorite dish is this holiday lamb, with well-chosen herbs and golden bread-crumb crust.

6½–7-pound whole leg of lamb (3–3¼ kg)
2 tablespoons butter, softened
1 teaspoon ground coriander
1 teaspoon tarragon
1 teaspoon basil
1 teaspoon dried parsley flakes
6 cloves garlic, crushed
1 cup dry white wine (¼ L)
½ cup dry red wine (1 dL)
1 cup beef stock (¼ L)
1 large onion, thinly sliced
2 eggs, beaten
½ cup dried bread crumbs (1 dL)
cayenne pepper to taste

Place the leg of lamb in a large roasting pan and rub the meat with the butter, coriander, tarragon, basil, parsley, and garlic. Pour the wines and stock over the lamb. Place the onion slices on and around the meat. Roast at 350°F (180°C) for 2–2¼ hours, basting every 25 minutes.

Remove the lamb from the oven (leaving the heat on) and paint it with the beaten eggs. Sprinkle on the bread crumbs, a little at a time, coating as much of the surface as possible. Return the lamb to the oven for several minutes until the crust is golden brown. Sprinkle with cayenne pepper. Let it stand for several minutes before slicing. In Trás-os-Montes this dish is served hot or cold, accompanied by millet patties.

Makloobeh

(Palestinian Lamb with Eggplant)

Serves 8

Harvard's Center for International Affairs resembles a mini–United Nations, with leaders from around the world rubbing elbows at the seminar table. Politicians from Korea, diplomats from Northern Ireland, and journalists from South Africa all become "research associates" when they enter Harvard's academic community. Among those working at the center is Walid Khalidi, a native of Jerusalem, whose research concerns the Middle East.

Khalidi, a spokesman for the Palestinians at Harvard and other Cambridge forums, is also loyal to Palestinian fare. Makloobeh (Arabic for "upside-down") is one of his favorite meals. The layered lamb and eggplant masterpiece is prepared in a deep pot, inverted onto a serving platter, and topped with pine nuts.

1½ cups vegetable oil (3½ dL)
5–6 onions, coarsely chopped
2 medium eggplants, peeled and cut into pieces
　　½-inch thick and 2 inches in diameter
1 pound lean lamb meat, cut into 1-inch pieces (46 dkg)
1 cup uncooked rice
2–3 cups beef broth or undiluted consommé (½–¾ L)
½ teaspoon cinnamon
½–1 teaspoon salt*
½ teaspoon pepper
　　pine nuts browned in olive oil for garnish
　　plain yogurt for topping

* If you use canned beef broth or consommé, cut way down on the salt.

(187)

Heat some of the oil in a deep pot. (Khalidi uses a Teflon-lined pot. Non-Teflon pots should be well greased.) Add the onions and cook over low heat, stirring frequently, until they are completely brown. Meanwhile, heat some of the remaining oil in a large skillet. Add the eggplant (in batches, if necessary) and cook over low heat, adding oil sparingly, as needed, until the eggplant is nearly soft. Remove the eggplant with a slotted spoon and drain it thoroughly on paper towels. Pat repeatedly with the towels to absorb as much oil as possible.

The lamb is cooked in the same pot as the onions. Remembering that the bottom layer of food in the pot becomes the top and most visible layer of the inverted makloobeh, you may choose to arrange the lamb and onions in a pattern. To do this, remove the onions. Cook the lamb over low heat for 10 minutes. Gather the cooked lamb pieces in the center and return the onions to the pot as a border around the lamb. *Or* push the cooked lamb toward the sides of the pot and place the onions in the center.

Place the eggplant on top of the cooked lamb and onions, smoothing with a spoon to form an even layer. Sprinkle the uncooked rice over the eggplant layer. Pour half of the beef broth or consommé into a bowl. Stir in the cinnamon, salt, and pepper. Pour this mixture into the pot. Add as much of the remaining liquid as needed to cover the rice by ½ inch. Bring to a boil over high heat. Cover, reduce the heat, and simmer 20–30 minutes, until all the liquid has been absorbed and the rice is tender.

Unmold the makloobeh onto a serving platter. Sprinkle the browned pine nuts on top. Serve with a dollop of yogurt or with a mixture of tahini, lemon juice, and chopped fresh parsley.

Swedish Lamb with Dill Sauce

Serves 8

W hen Sissela Bok earned her doctorate in philosophy at Harvard in 1970, she was investigating the ethics of voluntary euthanasia. Five years later, she joined the faculty of Harvard Medical School as a lecturer on medical ethics. Bok's latest research applies not only to medical decision-making but to a broad range of professional and interpersonal situations. *Lying* is the title and subject of her book.

Bok is a native of Stockholm, where this dish is served on special occasions. She now makes *dillkött på lamm* in her Cambridge home, where it is greatly appreciated by her husband, Derek Bok, the president of Harvard University.

> 5 pounds breast or shoulder of lamb, trimmed of fat
>   and cut into 2-inch pieces (2¼ kg)
> 8–10 sprigs dill
> 1 teaspoon salt
> 6 whole peppercorns

THE SAUCE

> 2 tablespoons butter
> 3 tablespoons flour
> ¼ cup chopped fresh dill (½ dL)
> 1 tablespoon white vinegar
> 1½ teaspoons sugar
> ½–1 teaspoon lemon juice
>   salt and pepper to taste
> 1 egg yolk, beaten
>   dill sprigs for garnish

(189)

Place the lamb (and the bones, if you have them, to add flavor to the stock) in a large pot or heavy casserole with the dill sprigs, salt, and whole peppercorns. Just cover with water and quickly bring to a boil over high heat. Lower the heat, skim the scum from the surface, and partially cover the pot. Simmer for 1–1½ hours, until the meat is tender. Remove the lamb to a serving bowl, reserving the stock. Cover the meat and keep it warm.

To make the dill sauce, strain the lamb stock and reduce it over high heat to 2½ cups (6 dL). Melt the butter in a large, deep skillet. Add the flour and stir to blend thoroughly. Remove the skillet from the heat. Add the lamb stock and whisk until the mixture is completely smooth. Return the skillet to the heat and quickly bring to a boil. Then reduce the heat and simmer for another 5 minutes. Add the chopped dill, vinegar, sugar, lemon juice, salt, and pepper. Remove the skillet from the heat and gradually pour in the beaten egg yolk, stirring constantly and vigorously. Return the skillet to a low heat and cook for several minutes, stirring constantly. (Do not let the sauce boil once the egg yolk has been added.) Pour the sauce over the meat and garnish with dill sprigs. Serve with boiled potatoes.

The Boks note that this dish freezes well and is tasty when reheated.

Honeyed Lamb with Fruit

Serves 4

Ann Coles, doctoral candidate at the Graduate School of Education, is a seasoned traveler. She first tasted this dish in Morocco, where it was served in an earthenware cooking vessel called a *tajine* (pronounced "ta-sheen"). There she learned to eat stew without silverware, using hard-crusted bread to scoop up the meat and soak up the juices. Coles also learned what to serve alongside. Try her Moroccan Chili-Tomato Salad as an accompaniment (p. 67).

⅓ cup olive oil (¾ dL)
2 large onions, thinly sliced
salt and pepper to taste
1 tablespoon minced fresh ginger or ½ teaspoon
powdered ginger
1 4-inch stick cinnamon or ½ teaspoon powdered
cinnamon
pinch of powdered saffron
2 pounds leg of lamb meat, trimmed of fat and cut into
1½-inch pieces (90 dkg)
12–16 pitted prunes or soaked, dried apricots
1 tablespoon honey
1 tablespoon lemon juice
2 tablespoons toasted white sesame seeds

Heat the oil in a large pot or heavy casserole. Add the onions, salt, pepper, ginger, cinnamon, and saffron. Add the lamb and stir to coat each piece with the onion mixture. Cover and simmer over low heat, stirring occasionally, for 1½ hours or until the meat is very tender.

Add the prunes or apricots, honey, and lemon juice. Stir, cover, and simmer for another 15 minutes. Sprinkle toasted sesame seeds on top just before serving.

Pork with Prunes in Sherry Sauce

Serves 4

As an administrative assistant at the Graduate School of Education, Nancy Brigham caters to both business and pleasure. First she balances budgets; then she plans parties — from weekly wine-and-cheese gatherings to annual Christmas extravaganzas.

Brigham's skills were recognized by an Ed School professor who invited her to cater a conference he was hosting. Since then she's become "Nancy Ellen Brigham: Purveyor of Palmary Parties." *Palmary*, as Brigham's business card points out, indicates something outstanding. Pork with prunes perpetuates the alliteration; the soy-sherry flavor merits the adjective.

  4 1-inch thick pork chops
  2 cooking apples, peeled, cored, and thinly sliced
  1 large onion, chopped
 12 pitted prunes, coarsely chopped
  1 cup sherry (¼ L)
 ½ cup water (1 dL)
  3 tablespoons soy sauce
  1 teaspoon ginger
 ¼ teaspoon garlic powder
  2 tablespoons flour
 ¼ cup water (½ dL)

Arrange 2 of the pork chops in the bottom of a lightly greased casserole or other heavy lidded vessel that can go from oven to stove top. Cover the chops with half the apples, onion, and prunes. Make a second layer in the same fashion. In a bowl, combine the sherry, ½ cup (1 dL) water, soy sauce, ginger, and garlic powder. Stir to blend thoroughly. Pour the mixture over the pork chops. Cover and bake at 350°F (180°C) for 50 minutes or until the meat is cooked through.

Place the casserole on the burner over low heat and uncover. Combine the flour and ¼ cup (½ dL) water and stir to blend thoroughly. Add to this mixture ½ cup (1 dL) hot juices from the casserole. Mix thoroughly and pour back into the casserole. Stir for about 4 minutes until the sauce thickens slightly. Place the pork chops on a serving platter and pour the sauce on top.

Pork Loin Roast with Herbs

Serves 8

The first press run at Harvard was in 1642, out of the home of College president Henry Dunster. The result was modest — *A List of Theses at the Commencement of Harvard College* — but it marked the beginning of an important publishing venture.

Now one of the largest university presses in the country, Harvard University Press occupies its own building near Radcliffe and publishes more than a hundred titles a year. The books cover subjects both of scholarly and of general interest, including *The Mussel Cookbook* and a series of short novels. About one third are written by Harvard faculty members.

Like most publishing houses, the Press receives requests to reprint information that appears in its books. Susan Metzger, permissions manager, handles these queries, including one from the author of this Harvard cookbook. Metzger granted permission ("world rights, in English") to reprint "Baked Stuffed Mussels," from *The Mussel Cookbook*, by Sarah Hurlburt. She also gave permission to include her own culinary specialty — a previously unpublished recipe for succulent pork roast.

1–2 cloves garlic
1 bay leaf
1 teaspoon salt
½ teaspoon sage
½ teaspoon rosemary
½ teaspoon basil
pepper
4 pounds boned, pork loin roast (1¾ kg) *
1 teaspoon salt
½ cup olive oil (1 dL)

Pound or chop the garlic, bay leaf, salt, sage, rosemary, basil, and pepper until they form a paste. The meat, once boned, will fall into two sections. Smear the herb paste on the larger section and arrange the second piece on top like a sandwich. Tie securely with white string in four or five places, carefully sealing the seasonings inside.

Place the roast in a large, heavy pot with water to cover and 1 teaspoon salt. (Bones may be included for additional flavor.) Cover and bring to a boil over high heat. Uncover and simmer for 1½ hours, turning once, and allowing the water to evaporate. (Liquid that remains in the pot after 1½ hours may be drained, skimmed of fat, and used as a flavoring in fried rice and sauces.) Paint the roast with olive oil and cook for 15 minutes, turning gradually, until the roast is brown on all sides. Place the roast on a serving platter, remove the strings, and let stand for several minutes before slicing.

* Ask your butcher to bone a 6-pound loin roast with ribs (2¾ kg). This will yield about 4 pounds of meat (1¾ kg).

Whipping up a little something in an eighteenth century kitchen. This book on the culinary arts was published in Amsterdam in 1709. The volume is housed in Harvard's Countway Medical Library.

Morsels of Pork

Serves 6

A Cuban restaurant in Washington, D.C., provided the inspiration for Dr. Jay Hayden's pork marinated in grapefruit juice. A member of the Class of 1962, Hayden is now an anesthesiologist at Boston University's Lahey Clinic. After work, he builds an appetite by long-distance running and bicycling. Then he satisfies his hunger with hearty dishes like this.

¼ cup grapefruit juice (½ dL)
¾ cup lemon juice (2 dL)
6 cloves garlic, pressed
¼ teaspoon ground cumin
¼ teaspoon oregano
1 teaspoon salt
3 pounds lean boneless pork, cut into chunks
   (1¼–1½ kg)
½ pound lard (23 dkg)
1 cup water (¼ L)

To make the marinade combine the juices and seasonings in a large bowl. Add the pork and stir to coat the pieces with the marinade. Cover and refrigerate overnight.

Place the lard and the water in a large, deep skillet and heat until the lard melts. Add the pork and marinade. Simmer over medium heat about 30–45 minutes, until most of the water and marinade have evaporated and the lard begins to make snapping noises. Raise the heat and cook until the meat turns brown, another 5–10 minutes. Serve with black beans and rice.

Fassumauru

(Sicilian Meat Loaf)

Serves 6–8

A professor of linguistics and chairman of his department, Karl V. Teeter studies Oriental and Native American languages. His extracurricular interest in Sicilian can be attributed to his wife, Anita, who taught him her family recipe for Sicilian meat loaf. Fassumauru resembles a paté with an assortment of fillings. Sliced cold it makes an attractive repast. Teeter also serves the loaf as a warm entrée, sliced and then simmered in a light tomato sauce.

THE MEAT LOAF

    ½ pound coarsely ground pork (23 dkg)
    2 pounds coarsely ground beef (90 dkg)
    2 eggs, lightly beaten
    ½ cup chopped fresh parsley (1 dL)
    ½ cup grated Romano cheese (1 dL)
    ½ cup dried French or Italian bread cubes (1 dL)
        salt and pepper to taste

THE FILLING

    2 hard-boiled eggs, quartered
    2 small onions, quartered
    2 ounces Provolone or Caciocavallo cheese, julienned (55 g)
    2 ounces prosciutto or Canadian bacon, julienned (55 g)
    2 ounces salt pork, rinsed and cut into thin strips (55 g)

Combine the ingredients for the meat loaf in a large bowl and mix thoroughly. Wet a ½-yard piece of cheesecloth, wring it dry, and place it horizontally on a flat work surface. Place the meat mixture on the cloth and press it into a rectangle about 18 by 36 inches and ½–¾ inch thick.

Arrange the filling horizontally across the center of the rectangle, leaving a 1-inch margin at both ends. Use the cheesecloth to help you lift the front long edge of the meat loaf and fold it backward over the filling. Peel back the cheesecloth but hold the meat in this position with one hand. Then bring the back long edge forward (again with the help of the cheesecloth) and carefully press it in to secure the filling inside the loaf. Wrap the cheesecloth over the loaf and twist the ends of the cloth until the roll is tight and compact. Refrigerate it overnight.

Remove the cheesecloth. Place the loaf in a large, deep roasting pan. Cook over high heat, turning carefully and gradually, until brown on all sides. Cover and simmer on the stove (or cook at 300°F, 150°C) for 2 hours. Remove the loaf and let it cool to room temperature. Refrigerate for 1 hour before slicing the loaf.

I Tatti Meatballs

Serves 8

Harvard owns no real estate on the French Riviera, but it does have a gorgeous villa in Italy. The Villa I Tatti, located near Florence, is surrounded by farmland and lovely gardens. Bequeathed to the University by alumnus Bernard Berenson, the villa houses his collection of medieval and Renaissance art, along with a library of 72,000 volumes.

Since 1961 the Villa I Tatti has welcomed a small group of scholars interested, as was Berenson, in the Italian Renaissance. These "fellows," who come from Harvard and other universities, eat and study at the Villa, but reside in Florence during their one-year fellowship.

Nello Nardi, who has long been the I Tatti chef, has filled many fellows with great Italian fare cooked with fresh produce from the Villa's own gardens. He is also known for a few Russian specialties, developed in honor of the late Nicky Mariano, Berenson's lifelong personal secretary and general facilitator of life at the villa. Mariano came originally from the Balkans, and Nello Nardi served this dish to remind her of home.

    2 tablespoons butter
    1 large onion, finely chopped
    1 pound ground pork (46 dkg)
    1 pound ground chicken (46 dkg) *
    1 pound ground veal (46 dkg)
    2 egg yolks, lightly beaten
 ½–1 cup grated Parmesan or Swiss cheese (1–2½ dL)
    ¼ cup chopped fresh parsley (½ dL)
    1 teaspoon salt
    ¼ teaspoon pepper
    ¼ cup flour (½ dL)
    ¾ cup light cream (1¾ dL)

Melt the butter in a large skillet. Add the onion and cook over medium heat until it turns clear. In a large bowl, combine the cooked onion with the ground meats, egg yolks, cheese, parsley, salt, and pepper. Mix thoroughly and roll into balls the size of walnuts. Dust them with flour and brown them (in batches, if necessary) in the skillet over medium-high heat. Reduce the heat and add the cream gradually. Simmer for 15 minutes or until the meat is cooked through. Serve with pasta.

* Ask your butcher to grind the chicken (and the other meats) for you, or grind them at home in a food processor.

Sweet-Sour Ham Loaf

Serves 6

F rom Lancaster County, Pennsylvania, home of shoo-fly pie, comes a cook with fond memories of old German-style cooking. Al Jacobs had this ham loaf every year for his birthday while he was growing up and now makes it himself in California. Jacobs, who studied at Harvard in the mid-fifties, teaches English at Menlo College. His tart, birthday ham loaf is well worth remembering on bland days that could do with some mark of distinction.

THE LOAF

    1½ pounds ground smoked ham (68 dkg)*
    1 pound ground pork (46 dkg)
    1 cup crushed crackers (¼ L)
    ½ cup milk (1 dL)
    2 eggs, lightly beaten
      pepper to taste

THE SAUCE

    1 cup brown sugar (¼ L)
    ⅓ cup vinegar (¾ dL)
    ½ teaspoon dry mustard
    ⅓ cup water (¾ dL)

Place the ground ham and pork in a large mixing bowl. Soak the crushed crackers in the milk. Add them to the meat mixture, along with the eggs and pepper. Stir to mix

---

* Ask your butcher to grind meats for you, or grind them at home using a food processor.

thoroughly. Place the mixture in a baking dish and pat it into a loaf shape.

To make the sauce, combine all the ingredients and stir until the sugar is dissolved. Bake the ham loaf at 350°F (180°C) for at least 1 hour, basting with the sauce every 10 minutes.

Astronautical Chili

Serves 4

Y ou can work up quite an appetite while walking on the moon, says one of the few who has been there and knows. Jack (Harrison) Schmitt, pilot for Apollo 17, spent twenty-two hours exploring lunar terrain. Back at the ship he refueled his system with rehydrated foods. (Inject water into a plastic package, knead, wait . . . *voilà!*) The menu on the moon ranged from stew to fruitcake, but Schmitt craved the spicier food from his native New Mexico.

These days Schmitt pilots a dusty red pickup, which he parks in the U.S. Senate garage. A former teaching fellow at Harvard (he took his Ph.D. in geology in 1964), Schmitt shifted smoothly from scientist-astronaut to politician. He is the ranking minority member of the Ethics Committee and a member of the Science and Transportation Committee, among others.

Schmitt has also made an impact on the culinary circles of Capitol Hill. His *very* hot chili (nicknamed "the out-to-launch special") tied for third place at a congressional cook-off. For the uninitiated, this chili may blast off the roof of the mouth. For hot chili veterans, it's a surefire hit.

This electric train "eliminates the need for a servant in the dining room" by serving the meal and then carting off the plates. The invention was announced in an 1887 issue of La Nature, found among the historic periodicals in Harvard's Science Center Library.

2 cups chili paste (½ L) *
1 cup cooked pinto beans and their liquid (¼ L)
1 pound lean ground pork or beef (46 dkg)
  rosemary to taste
  sage to taste
  pepper to taste
1 large green pepper, coarsely chopped
1 large tomato, coarsely chopped
1 large onion, coarsely chopped
  green chilis, minced
  salt to taste

* This astronomical quantity is *not* a typographical error; Senator Schmitt likes his chili to sizzle. Chili paste can be made by combining ground fresh chilis or chili powder with water. Various kinds of canned chili paste may be found in supermarkets and Oriental markets. Regardless of how much (or how little) chili paste or powder you decide to use, add enough additional water to make 2 cups (½ L).

In a large pot, combine the chili paste with the cooked pinto beans and their liquid. Let this simmer while preparing the ground meat.

Brown the ground pork or beef in a skillet, adding the rosemary, sage, and pepper. Add the contents of the skillet to the simmering beans and stir to mix thoroughly. Mix in the green pepper, tomato, and onion. Add green chilis and salt to taste. Simmer for at least 1 hour. Serve with tostados, corn chips, and plenty of cold drinks.

Bigos
(Polish Sauerkraut Stew with Rabbit and Sausage)

Serves 6

E very Wednesday Michael Harris attends the Harvard Number Theory Seminar. He sat in for four years while writing his thesis, "On p-Adic Representations Arising from Descent on Abelian Varieties Over Number Fields," and continued to attend after its completion in 1977. Harris is hard-pressed to explain in layman's terms what goes on at the seminar, or even the general thrust of his thesis topic. "I study number theory," he reports with a shrug, and even his close friends know little more than that.

Now an assistant professor of math at Brandeis University, Harris takes time off to attend math conferences in Europe. One side trip involved a sojourn in Poland, where bigos appeared regularly on every menu. Harris clung to the word like a trustworthy theorem, ordered bigos often, and was always pleased. Thankfully, the recipe is not very complicated and Harris found the formula easy to explain.

> 5 bacon strips
> 3 cloves garlic, pressed
> 1 medium onion, finely chopped
> 1 tablespoon paprika
> 1 pound rabbit meat, cut into 1-inch pieces (46 dkg) *
> 1 pound kielbasa or other sausage, sliced (46 dkg)
> 4 cups drained sauerkraut with liquid reserved (1 L)
> ¾ cup of the reserved sauerkraut liquid (1¾ dL)
> ¾ cup beer (1¾ dL)

Fry the bacon until it is crisp and set it aside. Pour the bacon grease into a large pot or heavy casserole. Add the garlic and onion and cook over medium heat until the onion turns clear. Reduce the heat. Add the paprika, rabbit, and sausage, and cook 10–15 minutes, stirring frequently. Add the sauerkraut, ½ cup (1 dL) of the reserved liquid, and beer. Simmer uncovered for 1 hour, adding sauerkraut liquid as needed to keep the mixture moist. Crumble the bacon and sprinkle it on top. Serve with rye bread.

* A 2½-pound (1¼ kg) domestic rabbit yields about 1 pound (46 dkg) of meat.

Faculty Club Horse Steak with Mushroom Sauce

Serves 4

C reative cooking was valued during World War II, when meat was rationed and budgets were tight. Julian Coolidge, then Faculty Club president, decided to try horse meat on the menu. He collaborated with a local dealer to secure the first shipment and soon offered horse in the lunch-dinner lineup.

After the war, horse was taken off the menu, but customers clamored for its return. Broiled horse steak has been offered at the Faculty Club ever since. Today the steaks come from North Platte, Nebraska, and are served in a sauce made by Faculty Club chefs. The sauce was designed to mask the flavor of horse meat. Used conservatively, it enhances ground beef and steak.

> 4 8-ounce horse steaks (4 23-dkg steaks)*
> vegetable oil
> 3 tablespoons butter
> 4 shallots or 1 small onion, finely chopped
> 2 cups thinly sliced mushrooms (½ L)
> ¼ cup Marsala or other sweet wine (½ dL)
> 2 beef boullion cubes
> 1½ cups tomato juice (3½ dL)
> 1 teaspoon liquid gravy enhancer
> salt and pepper to taste
> 1-2 teaspoons cornstarch
> 1 tablespoon cool water

* Available in some specialty stores or from the Central Packing Company, North Platte, Nebraska.

UN INVITÉ A UN DINER D'HIPPOPHAGES.

– Vous offrirai–je encore un peu ?..... c'est excellent n'est ce pas !....

A guest is offered a second helping of horse meat. This Daumier print holds a position of honor near the entrance to the dining room of the Harvard Faculty Club. Horse steak has been served at the Faculty Club for decades. The print, on "permanent loan" from the Fogg Art Museum, has announced that fact almost as long. (Courtesy of the Fogg Art Museum, Harvard University, Francis Calley Gray Collection. Gift of Frederick B. Deknatel.)

Pound the horse steaks with a mallet and soak them in vegetable oil for at least 2 hours.

To prepare the sauce, melt the butter in a saucepan. Add the shallots or onion and cook until golden. Add the mushrooms and cook just until they turn soft. Pour on the wine and cook over low heat for 15 minutes, stirring occasionally. Add the boullion cubes, tomato juice, gravy enhancer, salt, and pepper. Stir and simmer for another 15 minutes. Combine the cornstarch and the cool water, stirring to blend thoroughly. Add this mixture to the sauce, stir, and cook 3 minutes. Remove the sauce from the heat. Cover and keep warm.

Broil the horse steaks for 3 minutes on each side for rare, 5 minutes on each side for medium, and 7 minutes on each side for well done. Spoon the mushroom sauce on top. Use excess sauce over rice or mashed potatoes.

Fish and
Shellfish

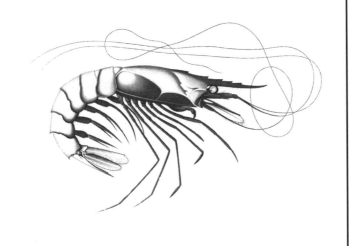

Boston's Best Schrod

Serves 1

H arvard Clubs may be found wherever Harvard alumni live, from Detroit to Lima, Seoul to Paris. The clubs, which design their own social and educational programs, exist in nearly 120 cities, but only one city boasts *two* Harvard Clubs, including one with a view of the University itself.

The old Harvard Club of Boston is located in Back Bay, where it looks out on the bustle of Commonwealth Avenue. The new club occupies the penthouse of a downtown high rise. Located at the very hub of "the Hub," this building commands a panoramic vista of Boston Harbor and an unobstructed view up the Charles River Basin. Seated at a table in the club's dining room, alumni can also view the tower of Harvard's Memorial Church and the white monolith of William James Hall.

From **Urbain Dubois's** Cuisine Artistique, *published in Paris in 1883 and housed at Radcliffe's Schlesinger Library.*

Both clubs share a recipe for what they consider the best schrod in Boston. From the old club, chef Ed Bonello explains how they prepare this hallowed New England specialty.

 2 tablespoons butter, softened
 ½ teaspoon chopped fresh parsley
 1 teaspoon lemon juice
   hot-pepper sauce to taste
   Worcestershire sauce to taste
 ½ pound cod fillet (23 dkg)
 ½ cup vegetable oil (1 dL)
 ¾ cup dried bread crumbs (1¾ dL)
   parsley sprigs and lemon wedges for garnish

In a small bowl, combine the softened butter, parsley, and lemon juice. Add the hot-pepper sauce and Worcestershire sauce. Whip the mixture with a fork and set it aside.

Preheat the broiler. Pat the cod with paper towels. Drench it in vegetable oil and coat both sides with bread crumbs. Place the cod in the hot broiler with the skin side facing up. Broil until the skin is firm, less than 3 minutes. Using a spatula, carefully turn over the cod. Broil the other side for several minutes until the cod is firm and golden brown. Lift the cod with a spatula and guide the serving plate underneath.

Spread the butter mixture on the "schrod." Garnish with parsley sprigs and lemon wedges.

Fish and Chips Casserole

Serves 4

Betsey Cogswell slept through her economics course in college, but now the field keeps her more than alert. Cogswell is the graduate secretary for Harvard's economics department, the largest department in the School of Arts and Sciences.

"Graduate secretary" means that Cogswell is the chief trouble-shooter when it comes to steering graduate students through Harvard's economics program. First she helps students register for courses. Later on she advises them on typing their theses, schedules their "orals," and sets up job interviews with recruiters. When the mother of a new Ph.D. spilled a martini on her son's diploma, Cogswell was the one who arranged for a duplicate to be made.

Born in Salem, Massachusetts (and, she claims, related to a witch), Cogswell is partial to down-home New England cooking. Her fish and chips casserole is a bit like

fish chowder, only layered, baked, and much more substantial.

> 3 tablespoons butter
> 1 large onion, thinly sliced
> 9 new potatoes, thinly sliced
>   salt and pepper to taste
> 1½ cups grated sharp cheddar cheese (3½ dL)
> 1½ pounds cod or haddock fillets (68 dkg)
> 1 cup milk or light cream (¼ L)
> ½ teaspoon rosemary
>   parsley sprigs and lemon wedges for garnish

Melt the butter in a large skillet. Add the onion slices and
cook until they turn clear. Add the potatoes and cook,
stirring occasionally, until they are nearly tender.

Place half the onions and potatoes in a lightly greased
baking dish. Season with salt and pepper. Sprinkle half
the cheese on top. Then make a layer of fish, using a
whole fillet or several large pieces. Pour on the milk or
cream and sprinkle with rosemary. Make another layer
with the remaining onions and potatoes. Season with salt
and pepper and sprinkle with the remaining cheese. Bake
at 350°F (180°C) for 20 minutes until the fish flakes
easily. Garnish with parsley and serve with lemon wedges.

Herbed Fish in Beer

Serves 4

With pickled herring as his standard breakfast,
it's obvious Kurt Krammer enjoys fish. Krammer, a native Austrian, manages the dining facilities in Kresge Hall at the Graduate School of Business

Administration, where he balances menus with a variety of entrées. At his own home, however, seafood predominates. His fish cooked in beer is made in the German style but flavored with a domestic brew.

2 pounds fillet of haddock or other white fish (90 dkg)
1 onion, thinly sliced
2 carrots, sliced
1 lemon
1 stick butter, melted
2 tablespoons wine vinegar
2 bay leaves
5 cloves
1 teaspoon dill
   salt and pepper to taste
¼–½ cup dried bread crumbs (½–1 dL)
1 12-ounce beer (3½ dL)
   parsley sprigs for garnish

Place the fish in a long baking dish. Lay the onion and carrot slices over the fish. Cut the lemon in half lengthwise, reserving half. Slice the other half and arrange the pieces on the fish. Pour the melted butter and vinegar over the fish. Add the bay leaves, cloves, dill, salt, and pepper.

Sprinkle the bread crumbs on top of the fish. Pour the beer into the baking dish until it covers no more than ¾ of the fish, leaving the bread crumbs dry. Cover with aluminum foil and bake at 350°F (180°C) for 40 minutes until the fish flakes. Garnish with parsley.

This dish may be served on a platter with young, parslied potatoes and cooked, sliced mushrooms. Krammer serves it with a salad made of Boston lettuce dressed with vinaigrette and finely chopped hard-boiled eggs.

Salmon Mousse

Serves 6

J oel Rosen was a Harvard undergraduate, on and off, for thirteen years before graduating in 1978. During his off years he worked as a printer's apprentice and later as the head of his own catering business.

As a caterer, Rosen has a distinctive style. He arrives at his client's home with groceries and a student staff, then cooks and designs platters using the client's accouterments. One well-received dish is this easy salmon mousse, which he serves in cold buffets or as an appetizer.

Rosen now has his hands full as a printer's assistant but still keeps a finger in the catering pie.

2 envelopes unflavored gelatin
¼ cup lemon juice (½ dL)
1 cup chicken broth (¼ L)

¼ cup vermouth (½ dL)
½ cup mayonnaise (1 dL)
¼ cup finely chopped Italian parsley (½ dL)
½ pint heavy cream, beaten thick but not stiff (¼ L)
2 tablespoons minced scallions
2 teaspoons Dijon mustard
2 teaspoons dill
½ teaspoon white pepper
    pinch of nutmeg

¾ cup finely chopped mushrooms, wrung dry in a cloth
    (1¾ dL)
1 cup shredded cucumber, drained of moisture (¼ L)
2 7-ounce cans salmon, drained and flaked (40 dkg
    total)

In a large bowl, combine the gelatin and lemon juice. Bring the chicken broth to a boil and pour it over the gelatin mixture. Stir until the gelatin is dissolved. Add the next group of ingredients (vermouth through nutmeg) and stir to blend thoroughly. Cover and refrigerate for 30 minutes or until the mixture has thickened slightly.

Beat the mixture until it is frothy. Add the mushrooms, cucumber, and salmon. Stir to mix well. Taste and adjust seasonings. Pour into a mold and refrigerate 2–3 hours, until set. Unmold onto a serving platter and garnish according to your fancy. For starters, Rosen suggests lemon wedges, black olives, and watercress or parsley.

Tuna-Parmesan Croquettes

Serves 6

Prosthetics is a required course for dental students at Harvard, and Dr. Tony Tolentino is their tour guide through the world of the crown and bridge. Assistant professor Tolentino instructs his students in the lecture hall and directs their work on patients in the Harvard Dental School clinic. He is also a chief of dentistry for the Harvard Community Health Plan, a medical care program for residents in the Boston-Cambridge area.

Tolentino, who himself sports several caps and crowns, notes that patients properly fitted with prosthetics can eat anything they want. His tuna croquettes, it so happens, are very easy on the mandibles. They're also fairly easy on the budget. This family recipe, deriving from Reggio di Calabria, Italy, turns tuna and leftover mashed potatoes into a flavorful meal.

2 7-ounce cans tuna, drained and flaked (40 dkg total)
2 cups mashed potatoes (½ L)
¼–½ cup grated Parmesan or Romano cheese (½–1 dL)
3 eggs, beaten
¼ cup chopped fresh parsley (½ dL)
1–3 cloves garlic, minced
salt and pepper to taste
1½ cups dried bread crumbs (3½ dL)
2½ cups vegetable oil (6 dL)

In a large bowl, combine the tuna, mashed potatoes, grated cheese, eggs, parsley, garlic, salt, and pepper. Mix thoroughly and shape into patties. Roll the patties in the bread crumbs. Heat the oil in a large, deep skillet and fry the croquettes on each side for several minutes, until golden brown. Drain them on paper towels.

Seafood Gumbo

Serves 16–20

Each December 27, no matter where he is, Dr. Joseph Henry has a big gumbo party. Henry, of Harvard's School of Dental Medicine, began the custom twenty years ago in his home town, the gumbo capital, New Orleans. This recipe produces one luscious gallon, the least Dr. Henry has made at one time. (One year he stirred up a full twenty-eight gallons.) His colleague Dr. Tony Tolentino, of the preceding recipe, paid Henry the ultimate tribute by downing eleven bowls at a single sitting.

Dr. Henry is chairman of the department of oral diagnosis as well as the affirmative action officer for the Dental

A Japanese greeting card featuring sea bream and lobster by nineteenth-century artist Totoya Hokkei. (Courtesy of the Fogg Art Museum, Harvard University, Duel Collection.)

School, which has three times the national average of women and minority students. A specialist in periodontics and endodontics, Dr. Henry treats patients requiring gum surgery and root canal work. The procedures he performs can be rather costly, as are the ingredients in his spicy gumbo. This dish, in fact, costs a small fortune to make. Like good dental care, it is worth the investment.

2 pounds mildly seasoned sausage (90 dkg)
1 cup finely chopped Bermuda onion (¼ L)
1 cup finely chopped celery (¼ L)
½ cup finely chopped pepper (1 dL)
1 pound medium or large shrimp, shelled (46 dkg)
1 cup cooked lobster meat, cut into chunks (¼ L)
1 pound seasoned, cooked crab meat (46 dkg)
2 pounds fresh, frozen, or canned okra (90 dkg)
1 cup sliced mushrooms (¼ L)
2 cups tomato sauce or condensed tomato soup (½ L)
1 8-ounce can cream of mushroom soup, undiluted
   (23 dkg)
1 cup ketchup (¼ L)
2 tablespoons sweet pickle relish
2 teaspoons hot-pepper sauce
1 tablespoon prepared mustard
5 bay leaves, crumbled
1 tablespoon sage
1 teaspoon paprika
1 teaspoon marjoram
1 teaspoon thyme
½ teaspoon monosodium glutamate
2 teaspoons pepper
2 teaspoons Old Bay Seafood Seasoning*
1 pint shucked oysters with their liquid (½ L)
   gumbo filé for garnish*

Fry the sausage in a large skillet, turning to brown on all sides. Remove it and drain on paper towels. Cook the chopped onion, celery, and pepper in the sausage grease (adding vegetable oil if needed) for 5 minutes, stirring occasionally. Remove them with a slotted spoon and set them aside. Fry the shrimp and lobster meat in the same

* Old Bay and gumbo filé are available in some supermarkets and gourmet shops. Old Bay adds a spicy flavor, which can also be accomplished by adding more hot-pepper sauce, pepper, mustard, or ginger. There is no real substitute for filé, the sassafras derivative that garnishes and thickens authentic gumbo. This recipe, however, is loaded with flavors and body, and so it will not suffer from one missing ingredient.

skillet until the shrimp are firm and pink and the lobster meat is firm. Place the contents of the skillet, along with the reserved onion mixture, in a pot that holds at least 5 quarts (4¾ L).

Slice the sausage into ½-inch pieces. Add to the pot the sausage and all remaining ingredients *except* the oysters and their liquid and gumbo filé. Stir to blend thoroughly. Add enough water to make 1 gallon. Bring the gumbo to a boil. Cover, reduce the heat, and simmer 4–6 hours, stirring occasionally. (Dr. Henry cooks his gumbo over an asbestos pad to prevent the gumbo from burning on the bottom of the pot.) Skim the grease from the surface. Add the oysters and their liquid and simmer for 30 minutes. Serve the gumbo over rice. Sprinkle gumbo filé on top of each serving.

Baked Stuffed Mussels

Serves 6

Inspired by the flavor and nutritional value of mussels, Graham Hurlburt took a leave-of-absence from the University to study mussel mariculture in Europe. When Hurlburt (Harvard's director of administrative services) and his wife Sarah returned, they began proselytizing for the valuable bivalve, which is high in protein and low in cholesterol. Graham noted in his report that an area the size of Cape Cod Bay (18 by 15 miles) could produce some 45 billion pounds of mussel meat each year. Sarah, meanwhile, had done some research of her own: her findings, entitled *The Mussel Cookbook,* were published by Harvard University Press.

Graham, who has since resumed his Harvard duties, now spends some of his free time tending the family's mussel crop at their South Shore home. Sarah is writing another book on seafoods that are underappreciated in this country. This one will provide American-style recipes for such "exotic" creatures as shark and squid. The Hurlburts remain partial to mussels, however, and this dish is one reason why.

> 3 pounds fresh mussels, cleaned and scrubbed (1¼–1½ kg)
> ½ cup dry white wine (1 dL)
> 4 tablespoons butter
> 3 tablespoons minced onion
> 3 tablespoons minced celery
> 1 tablespoon minced green pepper
> 3 tablespoons chopped fresh parsley
> ¾–1 cup cracker crumbs (2–2½ dL)
> hot-pepper sauce to taste
> salt to taste
> lemon wedges dusted with paprika for garnish

Place the clean mussels and white wine in a large, heavy pot. Cover and steam over high heat 5–7 minutes or until the shells open. When the mussels have cooled, remove the meats. Separate the shells at the hinge and set them aside. Strain the cooking liquid and set it aside. Finely chop the mussel meats.

Melt the butter in a skillet. Add the onion, celery, and green pepper. Cook over medium heat until the vegetables are soft. Remove the skillet from the heat. Add to the skillet the chopped mussels, parsley, cracker crumbs, hot-pepper sauce, and enough of the reserved cooking liquid to bind the mixture. Add the salt (and possibly lemon juice).

Spoon the mixture into the reserved mussel shells and arrange them on cookie sheets. Dot each with butter.

Bake at 450°F (230°C) for 15 minutes, until hot and light brown on top. Garnish the servings with paprika-dusted lemon wedges. This recipe, which serves 6 as an entrée, can also make dozens of elegant hors d'oeuvres.*

Oyster-Spinach Casserole

Serves 2

Elizabeth Pattullo approves salaries for Harvard graduate students who teach at the University — an occupation that is applauded by a thousand scholars yearly. From her busy office in the Radcliffe Quadrangle, Assistant Dean Pattullo directs the hiring of all "teaching fellows" for the Graduate School of Arts and Sciences. These fellows, or section leaders, personalize Harvard's large lecture courses by meeting regularly with small groups of students.

Pattullo, who administers a $3 million annual budget, finds that her work leaves her little time to cook. Across the campus, her husband, Edward L. Pattullo, is kept equally occupied by Harvard. He works at William James Hall, where he is director of the Center for Behavioral Sciences and a senior lecturer on psychology.

Given their schedules, the Pattullos thrive on the simplest of meals. Their oyster-spinach casserole makes a delicious quick supper for two. Using simple multiplication and four large baking dishes, they have expanded this recipe to serve forty guests.

* Reprinted by permission of the publishers from *The Mussel Cookbook* by Sarah Hurlburt, Cambridge, Mass.: Harvard University Press, Copyright © 1977 by the President and Fellows of Harvard College.

1 cup prepared bread stuffing (¼ L)
1 10-ounce package frozen chopped spinach, thawed
   (20 dkg)
2–3 tablespoons butter
2–4 tablespoons lemon juice
   salt and pepper to taste
½ pint shucked oysters, drained (¼ L)

Butter a small baking dish. Spread the dry stuffing in the bottom of the dish. Add the spinach to form a second layer. Dot with half the butter, sprinkle with some of the lemon juice, and season with salt and pepper. Place the oysters over the spinach layer. Top with the remaining butter and lemon juice, and season with salt and pepper. Bake at 375°F (190°C) for 12–18 minutes, until the oysters puff.

Scallop Ceviche with Ecuadorian Garnish

Serves 4

K en Miyata chases lizards through the rain forests of Ecuador. When he finally nabs one he measures its body. All this is done in the interest of science. Miyata, a graduate student in biology at Harvard, studies evolutionary diversity among *Anolis* lizards. This requires data not only on the animals' size, but on their habitats and diet as well.

Meanwhile, Miyata's own diet suffers while he's in the field. When the lizards and field-station food get him down, he heads for Quito and gorges himself. The first thing he orders is ceviche, a raw seafood cocktail "cooked" in the acid of a lime-lemon marinade.

Back in Cambridge, Miyata dries his soggy field notes in his office at the Museum of Comparative Zoology and recreates the ceviche in his nearby apartment. Although he substitutes New England scallops for the shrimp and conch used in Ecuador, he serves the dish with the authentic Ecuadorian garnish. It hisses and shrivels when tossed on ceviche and quickly absorbs the sharp flavors. In Cambridge as in Quito, the garnish is popcorn.

¾–1 cup lime and/or lemon juice (2–2½ dL)
¼ cup water (½ dL)
1 teaspoon vinegar
2 teaspoons hot-pepper sauce
1 clove garlic, pressed
⅓ cup minced red onion (¾ dL)

1 pound small sea scallops cut into ½-inch pieces or whole bay scallops (46 dkg)
lightly salted popcorn for garnish
chopped fresh parsley for garnish

To make the marinade combine the first group of ingredients in a large bowl and stir to mix thoroughly. Add the scallops and stir to coat with the marinade. Cover and refrigerate overnight.

Place the scallops and a little of the marinade in small bowls or scallop shells. Garnish with popcorn and parsley. Serve as a light summer lunch or as an hors d'oeuvre.

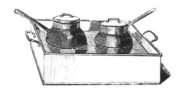

Scallops in White Sauce

Serves 2

H arvard is run by two governing bodies. The President and Fellows (also known as the Harvard Corporation) actually own and operate the University. They meet twice a month to conduct day-to-day business, including the appointment of faculty members.

Most of their decisions must be approved by the second body — the Board of Overseers, which works like the board of trustees at other universities. The thirty overseers, elected by alumni, meet at least six times a year. They approve the University's budget, advise on administrative policies, and keep tabs on academic departments through their visiting committees.

Both the President and Fellows and the Board of Overseers originated, with Harvard, in the seventeenth century. The year 1970 marked a new phase in their history. It was then that Helen Homans Gilbert (Class of 1936) was elected to the Board of Overseers. Gilbert was not only the first woman on the board, she was also the first woman to serve as its president.

Gilbert's tenure on the board has now ended, and she has more time to cook with her husband, Carl J. Gilbert (Law School 1931). He originated this dish of scallops, white sauce, and sherry, but notes that Helen Homans Gilbert helped it considerably.

    1 **pound scallops (46 dkg)**
¾–1 **cup white wine (2–2½ dL)**
       celery salt to taste

garlic salt to taste
cayenne pepper to taste
pepper to taste
2 tablespoons butter
2 tablespoons flour
½ cup milk (1 dL)
splash of sherry

Place the scallops in a saucepan with white wine to cover and add the seasonings. Simmer for several minutes until the scallops are firm and white. Remove the scallops with a slotted spoon (reserving the cooking liquid) and place them in a serving dish. Cover them and keep them warm. Drain the cooking liquid into a measuring cup.

Melt the butter in the saucepan. Add the flour and stir over low heat for several minutes, until slightly brown. Add ½ cup (1 dL) of the cooking liquid and the milk, whisking constantly until the sauce is thick and smooth. Add the sherry and stir until blended. Pour the sauce over the scallops. Serve over toast, English muffins, or rice.

Shrimp in Tarragon Sauce

Serves 4

Ever since his training as a professional French chef, Maurie Warren (Class of 1971) has been itching to open his own restaurant. This marvelous dish, which he developed while he was the chef at Le Bocage restaurant in Cambridge, will soon be featured at his own Chez Mon Cher. Warren is particularly fond of its flavor and decided, just this once, to share a chef's secret.

Le Maître d'hotel *by Antonin Carême is counted among the culinary treasures at Radcliffe's Schlesinger Library. Published in Paris in 1822, the book bears this frontispiece showing the similarity of costumes for chefs "ancien et moderne."*

½ cup white wine (1 dL)
   juice of 1 lemon
 3 tablespoons finely chopped shallots
 1 tablespoon tarragon
¼ teaspoon salt
 3 sticks sweet butter, softened
   salt and white pepper to taste
   cayenne pepper to taste
32 medium shrimp, shelled and deveined

In a saucepan, combine the wine, lemon juice, shallots, tarragon, and salt. Reduce the mixture over medium heat until nearly dry. Adjust the heat to very low and gradually whisk in 2 of the sticks of butter. When the sauce is thick and creamy, taste and season with salt, white pepper, and cayenne pepper. Cover the saucepan and remove it from the heat.

Melt the remaining butter in a skillet. Add the shrimp and cook over low heat for several minutes, until they are firm and pink. Remove the shrimp with a slotted spoon and add them to the sauce. Serve the dish with rice, French bread, and a bottle of Blanc de Blanc. For the complete meal, chef Warren suggests an hors d'oeuvre of cold, blanched asparagus with orange sauce or vinaigrette, and a dessert of cheese and fruit.

Bobó de Camarão
(Brazilian Shrimp with Coriander)

Serves 6

Five million immigrants representing forty-five nationalities have arrived in Brazil since the turn of the century. Naomi Moniz, a native of São Paulo and a graduate student in Romance languages at Harvard, studies the literatures of these immigrant groups.

Because much of her research is done in Brazil, Moniz can actually *taste* the impact of immigrant cultures. Italians have had the greatest influence, she says, bringing pasta and pizza to the Brazilian diet.

Brazilian cookery is peppered with a few African dishes as well. Bobó, common in Baía (a state in northeastern Brazil), has roots in an African bean dish called "bovo." The Brazilian influence is seen through the omission of beans and the addition of shrimp and coconut milk.

> 1 pound manioc root (46 dkg)*
> 1 cup water (¼ L)
> ¼ cup vegetable oil (½ dL)
> 2 onions, finely chopped
> 2–3 tomatoes, halved and seeded
> 2 tablespoons chopped fresh coriander leaves*
> salt to taste
> 1 teaspoon pepper
> 2 pounds medium shrimp, shelled and deveined
>   (90 dkg)
> 1 cup unsweetened coconut milk (¼ L)*
> ¼ cup coconut oil (½ dL)*

* Some of bobó's ingredients may be unfamiliar but the dish is well worth some investigative shopping, and the items, once purchased, are fun to have around. Manioc, or cassava (the plant from which tapioca is derived) may be found fresh or frozen in Latin American stores.

While there, ask for the leaves of fresh coriander — cilantro. (This herb is also sold in Indian and Italian markets and in Oriental markets where it's called Chinese parsley. Excess coriander may be added to curries, sausage, or guacamole.)

Unsweetened coconut milk, available in Latin American and Oriental markets, is also called for in the recipe on page 59.

Coconut oil, found in Latin American and some gourmet shops, adds interest to all kinds of entrées. Try it mixed with lime juice when frying scallops and fillets of fish or chicken.

(230)

Peel the manioc and cut it into chunks. Boil it in salted water 12–15 minutes, until it is tender. Drain the manioc and purée it in a blender, gradually adding the water until the mixture is smooth. Set it aside.

Heat the vegetable oil in a large, deep skillet or heavy casserole. Add the onions and cook them until they turn golden. Add the tomatoes, coriander leaves, salt, and pepper. Cook over medium heat for 10 minutes, stirring occasionally. Add the shrimp, manioc purée, coconut milk, and coconut oil, stirring to mix thoroughly. Cook over medium heat until the shrimp are firm and pink and the mixture begins to boil.

Stir-Fried Shrimp

Serves 4

When Ellen Schrecker (Class of 1960, Ph.D. 1974) was a student of Chinese culture in Taiwan, part of her education was of a culinary sort. One of her teachers returned with her to the States, where she collaborated with Ellen and John Schrecker in compiling *Mrs. Chiang's Szechwan Cookbook*. Another of Schrecker's tutors, also Szechwanese, taught her this method of cooking large, unshelled prawns. When Schrecker returned to her own culture — and markets — she adapted the recipe to the largest shrimp that her budget would allow.

Now a fellow at Radcliffe's Institute for Independent Study, Schrecker is conducting research on McCarthyism in academe. She is also a preceptor in expository writing at Harvard — and a noted Cambridge master of Szechwan cuisine.

    1 pound large shrimp (46 dkg)
    ¼ cup peanut oil (½ dL)
    ½ teaspoon salt
    5 cloves garlic, minced
    1 tablespoon minced fresh ginger
    2 tablespoons rice wine vinegar*
    3 tablespoons soy sauce
    1 tablespoon sugar
    6 scallions, minced

Wash the shrimp. Remove the legs but keep the shells intact. Prepare and measure all ingredients and place them within arm's reach of the stove. In a small bowl, combine the rice wine vinegar, soy sauce, and sugar, stirring to blend thoroughly.

Place a wok or heavy skillet over high heat for 20 seconds before adding the peanut oil. Heat the oil for 30 seconds and then toss in the shrimp, sprinkle with the salt, and stir-fry for 3 minutes. Add the garlic, ginger, and the vinegar sauce. Cover and cook for 2 minutes. Add the scallions and stir-fry for 30 seconds. Serve with boiled rice.

Shrimp Louisiane

Serves 6

When he was eighteen years old, Jimmy Elow left the bayou and traveled to Boston in search of work. He found a job as a bus boy at the Harvard Faculty Club, and two decades later he is still on the

* Rice wine vinegar can be found in Oriental markets and some gourmet shops.

staff. These days, with a chef's hat flopping over one eye, Elow confides that he's one of the best at Harvard. Club diners fond of hot curries agree — as do Elow's fellow kitchen workers, who call him the Black Prince. But Elow is willing to give credit where it's due. This dish, one of the most popular on the Faculty Club menu, is actually a legacy from Jimmy Elow's mother.

½ pound salt pork, finely chopped (23 dkg)
2 onions, coarsely chopped
1 clove garlic, minced
2 large green peppers, cut into 1½-inch pieces
½ pound mushrooms, sliced (23 dkg)
½ teaspoon thyme
½ teaspoon oregano
½ teaspoon basil
½–2 teaspoons cayenne pepper
3 pounds shrimp, shelled and deveined (1½ kg)
1 6-ounce can tomato paste (17 dkg)
1 1-pound can stewed tomatoes (46 dkg)
2 cups sliced fresh or frozen okra (½ L)

In a large pot, combine the salt pork, onions, garlic, peppers, and mushrooms. Add the thyme, oregano, basil, and cayenne. Cook over medium heat for 10 minutes, stirring occasionally. Add the shrimp, tomato paste, and stewed tomatoes. Simmer for 30 minutes, stirring frequently. Add the okra and simmer 5–10 minutes, until the okra is tender. Serve with boiled rice.

Snacks and Trimmings

Peaceable Sandwich

Serves 2

Father Carney Gavin works among mummies and tombstones in his Harvard workshop, the Semitic Museum. As curator of Near Eastern art and archaeology, Gavin cares for and adds to this collection of relics. His own archaeological research, conducted in the Fertile Crescent, involves scavenging for artifacts from the second millennium B.C. His favorite finds are tablets bearing cylinder seals (stylized impressions that serve as the author's signature), which yield clues to the customs and beliefs of those times.

For most of the year, Gavin dines on Lithuanian food prepared by the cook at the rectory of St. Columbkille's Parish in Brighton. Occasionally, however, he eats with friends in Cambridge. One spring, Gavin attended a Seder, where he relished his first taste of gefilte fish. During digs, of course, he eats Near Eastern foods like pita

"Pancake Woman," an etching by Rembrandt. (Courtesy of the Fogg Art Museum, Harvard University, Francis Calley Gray Collection. Gift of Frederick B. Deknatel.)

bread and chick peas. Eager for unity among various Near Eastern factions, Father Gavin developed this sandwich "in the spirit of peace."

2 large pieces gefilte fish, cut into 1-inch pieces*
¾ cup cooked chick peas, drained (1¾ dL)
¼ cup chopped chives or scallion greens (½ dL)
¼ cup chopped cucumber (½ dL)
¼ cup plain yogurt (½ dL)
¼ cup sour cream (½ dL)
¼ teaspoon thyme
1 large loaf pita or Syrian bread

In a bowl, combine the gefilte fish, chick peas,. chives or scallion greens, and cucumber. In a separate container, combine the yogurt, sour cream, and thyme. Cut the pita in half and open each piece to form a pocket. Pour some of the yogurt mixture into each half, lightly coating both sides. Spoon half the gefilte fish mixture into each bread pocket. Top with the remaining yogurt dressing and an extra dash of thyme. This sandwich can be supplemented with chopped tomatoes and scallion bulbs.

Congyou Bing

(Chinese Scallion Pancakes)

Makes 10 small pancakes

Founded in 1873 as a news-literary weekly, *The Harvard Crimson* is now Cambridge's only "breakfast-table daily." Over the years it has increased its news coverage and has become known for its pungent editorials and its scoops on University events.

* To make your own gefilte fish, see p. 9.

As director of the newspaper's photography staff, Lisa Hsia (Class of 1980) helps foster a tradition of innovative photojournalism. As a cook, she adheres to her Chinese heritage. Congyou bing, Hsia reports, "are something Chinese peasants eat all the time."

    2 cups sifted flour (½ L)
    ⅔ cup boiling water (1½ dL)
  3–4 scallions, minced
    1 cup vegetable oil or other cooking oil (¼ L)
  1–2 tablespoons coarse salt

Place the flour in a large bowl. Add the boiling water and stir until the mixture is cool enough to handle. Turn out onto a lightly floured surface. Knead until it forms a sticky dough. Roll the dough into a ball and place it in a bowl. Cover it and let it stand for 20 minutes.

Divide the dough in half. Then divide each half into 5 equal pieces. Roll each piece into a ball. Then flatten each with a rolling pin to form a 3–4-inch circle. Using a pastry brush, lightly brush each circle with a little of the oil. Sprinkle the scallions and salt in the center of each circle, leaving a narrow margin all the way around. Roll up the circles, tucking in the filling at the ends as you roll, and pinching the ends closed to keep the filling inside. Wind each roll into a coil and flatten to form a 4–5-inch circle.

Heat the remaining oil in a large, deep skillet. Fry the pancakes for about 2 minutes on each side, until golden brown. Drain them on paper towels. Serve warm as they are or with a dip of Chinese duck sauce.

Orange-Almond Rice Pilaf

Serves 8

D an Jones is the photographic archivist at Harvard's Peabody Museum of Archaeology and Ethnology, where he tends a vast collection of photographs. Most of the prints document Peabody expeditions, showing pots and shards recovered on digs in the Middle East or contemporary artifacts from Oceanic cultures.

Jones began his career in photography at a New York studio that focused on food. He still has an eye — and a taste — for the art. This pilaf mosaic (yellow rice, red pepper, brown almonds, green parsley) is lovely to look at and even nicer to eat.

1–3	cloves garlic
12	whole cardamom seeds
12	whole cloves
1	1-inch stick cinnamon
3	tablespoons peanut oil or safflower oil
1	onion, finely chopped
2	tablespoons finely chopped sweet red pepper
1½	cups uncooked long-grain rice (3½ dL)
1½	cups chicken broth (3½ dL)
½	cup orange juice (1 dL)
2	tablespoons honey
2	teaspoons grated orange rind
1	teaspoon salt
¼	cup toasted slivered almonds (½ dL)
1	cup chopped celery (¼ L)
½	cup seedless golden raisins (1 dL)
½	teaspoon turmeric

parsley sprigs for garnish

Place the garlic, cardamom, cloves, and cinnamon in a tea ball or wrap them loosely in cheesecloth and tie with white string.

Heat the oil in a large, deep skillet or a pot. Add the onion and pepper and cook over medium heat for 5 minutes. Add the rice and continue cooking for 5 minutes, stirring constantly. Add the ball of seasonings, along with all remaining ingredients except the parsley. Bring to a boil over high heat. Reduce the heat, cover, and simmer for 25 minutes or until all the liquid has been absorbed and the rice is tender. Remove the ball of seasonings. Garnish with parsley.

Serve with roast lamb or other entrées that are seasoned simply.

Leema Mehtayha

(Moroccan Pickled Lemon)

"Some of the best cooks in the country are philosophers and logicians," reasons Hilary Putnam, Walter Beverly Pearson Professor of Modern Mathematics and Mathematical Logic. Putnam refers especially to his colleagues in Ann Arbor (known in some circles as the Cambridge of the Midwest), who once formed a society devoted to dialogue and recipes.

Members of Esophagus Logico-Philosophicus taught Putnam several recipes, including this one for Moroccan pickled lemon. Leema mehtayha is actually an ingredient, not a dish in itself, and may be added to sauces and salad dressings. In Morocco it is used with beef or chicken cooked with green olives and turmeric.

10 lemons
⅓ cup salt (¾ dL)
water

Quarter the lemons and squeeze the juice into a bowl. Discard the seeds. Place the lemon rinds, lemon juice, and salt in a large jar. Add water to cover. Seal and let stand for 1 month.

To use the lemons in cooking, remove several slices of the pickled lemon and rinse off the salt. Scrape off and discard the pulp. Mince the rind or whirl it in a blender. Putnam uses this ingredient in a simple deglazing sauce for chicken or whenever a sharp, pickled flavor is appropriate. For starters try a dash in the Moroccan lamb stew on page 190.

Water Chestnut Stuffing for Turkey
Stuffs a 12-pound turkey

As author of *The Enriched, Fortified, Concentrated, Country-Fresh, Lip-Smacking, Finger-Licking, International, Unexpurgated Foodbook,* James Trager *should* be an authority on food. A 1945 graduate of Harvard College, Trager began his treatise with a discussion of Adam's apple (possibly an apricot, or, as the Koran claims, a banana) and ended with an essay on food franchises and chemical additives.

As if that weren't enough, Trager went on to compile *The Big, Fertile, Rumbling, Cast-Iron, Growling, Aching,*

Unbuttoned Bellybook (about world hunger and nutrition) and *The Great Grain Robbery* (about the 1972 Russian wheat deal).

Despite the thousands of pages he has written about food, Trager is a humble cook who follows other people's recipes. His only creation is this stuffing for turkey. The dish was invented one Thanksgiving when someone forgot to buy chestnuts for a more traditional stuffing.

> 2 tablespoons butter
> 1 onion, chopped
> ½ pound sausage meat, removed from the casing (23 dkg)
> 1 cup beef broth (¼ L)
> 1 teaspoon chopped chives
> 1 teaspoon chopped fresh parsley
> ½ teaspoon thyme
> ¼ teaspoon marjoram
>   salt and pepper to taste
> 2 cups water chestnuts, drained and coarsely chopped (½ L)
> 4 cups dried bread cubes (1 L)
> ½ cup cognac (1 dL)

Melt the butter in a large, deep skillet. Add the onion and cook until it turns golden. Add the sausage, beef broth, chives, parsley, and seasonings. Cook over medium heat for 5 minutes, stirring constantly. Add the water chestnuts, bread cubes, and cognac. Stir and cook for another 5 minutes. Remove the skillet from the heat and let the mixture cool.

Stuff the turkey just prior to roasting (to prevent spoilage). Loosely pack the stuffing into the turkey cavity. Use excess stuffing to stuff the breast.

Chirmol

(Guatemalan Tomato-Mint Sauce)

Makes about 1½ cups

The Cachikel Indians of San Martín Jilotepeque, Guatemala, believe that wild mint has medicinal value. They tuck the *hierba buena* ("good herb") in their hats as a remedy for headache. For stomach pain, they slip it under their belts. For all-around good health, they use it in cooking. This chirmol is made with mint, tomatoes, and hot peppers. The Cachikel use it to flavor their daily cornmeal mush and to top the broiled meats they have on special occasions.

Lawrence Cohan lived with the Cachikel in their Guatemalan village when he was a Harvard medical student doing an internship in rural health. He used modern drugs and techniques in his work, while learning what he could about local folk medicine. Chirmol was one lesson he learned very well.

Now a pediatrician at Massachusetts General Hospital in Boston, Dr. Cohan serves chirmol over broiled beef and chicken. When chilled, the sauce becomes a fiery dip for corn chips.

> 3 ripe tomatoes
> 2 tablespoons chopped fresh mint or ½ tablespoon
>   dried spearmint
> 1 onion, finely chopped
> 1–2 dried red peppers, crumbled*
>   salt to taste

* After crumbling the peppers, be sure not to touch your eyes or face until you have washed your hands, as the peppers can cause a burning sensation.

Place the tomatoes in a baking dish and sprinkle them with the mint, onion, and peppers. Bake at 400°F (205°C) for 15–30 minutes, until the tomatoes burst. Let them cool slightly; then mash and blend thoroughly. Add salt to taste.

Pear-Ginger Conserve

Makes about 3 pints

Students living in the Radcliffe residences appreciate Hilles Library, with its cinema, penthouse coffee shop, and 137,000 volumes. Among these books are the required reading materials for all undergraduate courses. As the public services librarian, Pat Hall (a 1967 graduate of the Harvard Extension School) maintains this "12,000-item, closed reserve system" that saves Hilles regulars from frosty winter walks to Widener Library.

Hilles (where Jenny meets Oliver in Erich Segal's *Love Story*) is situated on the southwest corner of the Radcliffe Quadrangle. Walking through the quad to get to and from work, Hall must pass by a cluster of pear trees. Around Labor Day, when the fruit falls to the ground, she gathers the pears for this sweet, nutty conserve.

    8 cups chopped pears (2 L)
4½ cups sugar (1 L)
    2 tablespoons ginger
    1 lemon
    1 8¼-ounce can crushed pineapple (23 dkg)
    1 cup chopped walnuts or slivered almonds (¼ L)

Cut the pears into pieces about the size you would like to see on your morning toast. Place them in a large bowl with the sugar and ginger. Toss and then let stand for 30 minutes. Place the mixture in a large pot and slowly bring to a boil. Reduce the heat and simmer for 15 minutes, stirring frequently. Slice the lemon into sections, removing the seeds and the tough white membranes. Chop what remains of the lemon, peel and all, into tiny pieces. Add the lemon bits and crushed pineapple to the pear-sugar mixture. Simmer for about 30 minutes, stirring frequently, until the mixture thickens. Add the nuts and stir to mix thoroughly. Pour into sterilized jars.

Date-Raisin Chutney

Makes about 2 pints

M onkeys are the business of microbiologist Muthiah Daniel of the New England Regional Primate Center. Like most of the scientists at this Harvard facility, Daniel studies diseases that plague monkeys and people. With his associates he has isolated two cancer viruses and is developing chemotherapies to thwart or prevent them. Daniel also investigates the herpes viruses through research on South American owl monkeys and marmosets. His subjects are among the one thousand primates found at the center, which is located some thirty miles west of Cambridge in Southboro.

Muthiah Daniel and his wife Ria are natives of Sri Lanka (formerly Ceylon) — where hot curried dishes prevail in the kitchen. Their authentic chutney, served as a condiment for curries, contains a powerful dose of vinegar. Feel free to experiment with the quantity of sugar suggested — more may be required to please the Western palate.

        2 cups cider vinegar (½ L)
        1 cup water (¼ L)
    4–6 cloves garlic, minced
        1 tablespoon minced fresh ginger
        1 teaspoon chili powder
    ½–¾ cup brown sugar (1–2 dL)
        1 pound pitted dates, chopped (46 dkg)
        1 cup raisins, chopped (¼ L)

In a blender, whirl the vinegar, water, garlic, ginger, and chili powder. Place the mixture in a large saucepan, add the sugar, and bring to a boil. Reduce the heat and simmer for 5 minutes, stirring occasionally. Add the dates and raisins, return the heat to high, and continue stirring until the mixture boils. Reduce the heat and simmer for 15–20 minutes, stirring constantly. Taste to see if more sugar is needed. Place the chutney in sterilized bottles and store in the refrigerator.

Serve it with chicken curry, roast beef, or lamb, or spread it on bread and butter for a snack. Chutney also makes a good dip for Indian Spinach Pakoras, page 27.

Desserts

[OVERLEAF] *Another illustration from* Cuisine de tous les pays, *by Urbain Dubois. The nineteenth-century volume is housed at Radcliffe's Schlesinger Library.*

Palatschinken Torte

(Austrian Crepe Torte)

Makes an 8-inch torte

When a new work of art joins the Fogg Art Museum collection, Lisa Ronis is one of the first to know. Every piece pays an early visit to the Fogg photo department, where Ronis arranges for it to be photographed before it is hung or mounted. The photo, with its negative, is then stored in Ronis's vast complex of filing cabinets.

These photo files document more than new acquisitions. Ronis keeps a "before and after" record of ailing masterpieces that undergo repairs or restoration in the conservation department. She also handles photographic services for the museum. She scheduled the "shootings" and provided the photo prints for the Fogg reproductions that help decorate this book.

Ronis's culinary contribution is a three-dimensional

masterpiece: fifteen palatschinken (the Austrian version of crepes) alternated with raspberry preserves and a cheese-raisin filling.

THE PALATSCHINKEN

1¾ cups flour (4 dL)
2 cups milk (½ L)
2 eggs, lightly beaten
¼ cup sugar (½ dL)
  dash of salt
3 tablespoons vegetable oil

For this dish you will need a crepe pan and a round baking dish with the same circumference. An 8-inch crepe pan or skillet and an 8-inch Pyrex soufflé dish are ideal. The baking dish should be at least 3 inches deep, and Pyrex will show off the beauty of the layered torte.

To make the palatschinken, combine the flour and milk in a large bowl and beat until smooth. Add the eggs, sugar, and salt. Stir to blend thoroughly. Heat a little of the oil in the crepe pan or skillet. Pour a thin layer of batter into the pan and cook for several minutes on each side until golden. Use all the batter, making 12–15 palatschinken. Set them aside while preparing the filling.

THE FILLING

½ pound farmer cheese (23 dkg)
½ pound pot cheese (23 dkg)*
½ cup golden raisins (1 dL)
¼ cup sugar (½ dL)
3 egg yolks, beaten
1 teaspoon lemon juice
1 8-ounce jar raspberry, plum, or other preserves
  (23 dkg)

* Or use a total of 1 pound farmer cheese (46 dkg).

Combine all the ingredients for the filling except the preserves, and stir to mix thoroughly. The mixture will be lumpy.

Place a single palatschinke in the bottom of the lightly greased baking dish. Cover with a thin layer of preserves. Lay the second palatschinke on top and cover with a layer of the cheese-raisin filling. Continue alternating palatschinken with layers of preserves and the cheese-raisin filling until they have all been used.

THE TOPPINGS

    1 cup sour cream (¼ L)
    ¼ cup sugar (½ dL)
       maraschino cherries
       toasted slivered almonds

Blend the sour cream and sugar. Spread this evenly on top of the torte. Bake at 350°F (180°C) for 20 minutes until the topping is light brown. Let the torte cool before decorating the surface with cherries and almonds.

Chocolate Torte with Mocha Frosting

Makes a 9-inch torte

The flora at Harvard's Gray Herbarium come from all over the world. The specimens fill cabinets on the building's top floor, but processing begins in the basement, where Edith Hollender works.

Hollender, born in Czechoslovakia, works with several other women whose job is to mount plants and identifica-

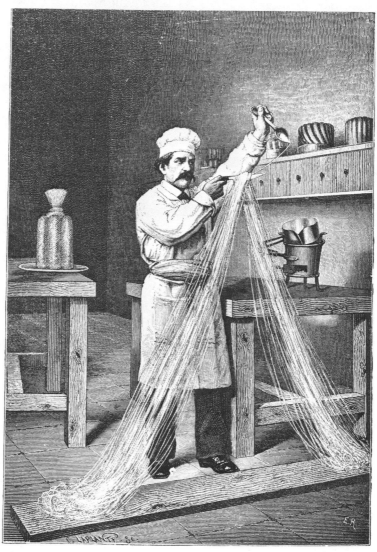

"*Spinning Sugar*" *from* The Royal Book of Pastry and Confectionary, *by Jules Gouffé. Published in London in 1874, this book can be found at the Schlesinger Library at Radcliffe.*

tion labels on paper for storage. She sometimes translates letters from Czech and Hungarian botanists and once discovered a good Sachertorte recipe in a newspaper wrapped around an Australian plant. Mostly, however, her work is repetitive, so she and her colleagues take a break every afternoon to sample each other's culinary experiments. After work, Hollender feeds her mind by studying nutrition at the Harvard Extension School.

Here is the torte that is most appreciated by her colleagues. It even lures botanists from the upper floors.

THE TORTE

    8 large eggs, separated
  ¾ cup sugar (1¾ dL)
    4 teaspoons cocoa
1⅓ cups walnut meats (3¼ dL)

Line the bottom and sides of a 9-inch spring-form pan with waxed paper. The side panel should extend 1 inch above the top of the pan. Grease the waxed paper with butter or oil. Cream the egg yolks and sugar. Add the cocoa and beat to blend thoroughly. Using a hand-held rotary grater, process the walnut meats until they are light and powdery. (Hollender does not advocate using a food processor or blender for this procedure.) Stir this into the cocoa mixture. Beat the egg whites until they form stiff peaks. Stir ⅓ of the beaten egg whites into the mixture before gently folding in the rest.

Pour the batter into the prepared cake pan and bake at 350°F (180°C) for 1 hour. Remove the cake from the oven and let it stand for 3 minutes. Remove the pan and the waxed paper, and let the cake cool thoroughly. (Hollender places hers on a splatter screen supported by three cans so both the top and bottom can cool at once. She warns that the cake is too delicate to rest on a regular cooling rack.)

THE FROSTING

2 large eggs, lightly beaten
¾ cup sugar (1¾ dL)
4 teaspoons cocoa
1 teaspoon instant coffee
2 sticks unsalted butter

Combine the beaten eggs and the sugar in a saucepan. Cook over very low heat for 10 minutes, stirring vigorously and constantly until thick and white. Add the cocoa and coffee. Continue stirring and cooking for 3 minutes. Remove the saucepan from the heat. Add the butter and stir until it melts. Cover the frosting and refrigerate it for 1 hour. Beat it until light and creamy before frosting the torte.

THE TOPPINGS

3 tablespoons apricot preserves
3 tablespoons maraschino cherries, drained
¼ cup whipped cream (½ dL)

When you are ready to construct the torte, slice the cake into three layers using a sharp chef's knife. Hollender first makes a cut about 1 inch deep all the way around the cake before slicing through.

Ice the bottom layer with mocha frosting, the middle layer with apricot preserves, and the top and sides with the remaining mocha frosting. Decorate the surface with maraschino cherries and whipped cream swirls.

First-timers are sometimes intimidated by the prospect of slicing this small cake into three layers. If you chicken out, two layers are fine. Use the apricot preserves in between the two layers. Top with the mocha frosting, whipped cream, and cherries.

Cranberry Sour Cream Cake

Makes a 9-by-13-inch cake

D an A. Del Vecchio is one of a very few nonstudent employees at Harvard Student Agencies, which has distributed $3 million in student wages since its establishment in 1957. As manager, Del Vecchio supervises the Agencies' enterprises, from the weekly linen service to disco dance lessons.

Del Vecchio is particularly interested in the Agencies' projects that relate to food and drink. Among them are a catering service staffed by student chefs and a bartending course taught by students who confer the Harvard "Masters of Mixology" degree.

But Del Vecchio's interest in culinary matters is not strictly business. In his own kitchen he likes to invent desserts. In this simple creation he uses cranberries from Massachusetts, where most of the nation's fresh cranberries are packaged. Eaten plain, this cake is nearly a bread. With whipped cream or frosting it's a proper dessert.

    1 stick butter
    1 cup sugar (¼ L)
    2 eggs, beaten
    2 teaspoons vanilla
    1 teaspoon baking powder
    1 teaspoon baking soda
    ½ teaspoon salt
    2 cups sifted flour (½ L)
    1 cup sour cream (¼ L)
    2½ cups cranberries, chopped (6 dL)
    1 cup chopped walnuts (¼ L)

In a large bowl, cream the butter and sugar. Add the eggs and vanilla and stir to blend thoroughly. Stir in the baking powder, baking soda, and salt. Gradually add the flour, alternating with the sour cream. Fold in the cranberries and walnuts.

Pour the batter into a greased and floured 9-by-13-inch baking pan. Bake at 350°F (180°C) for 45 minutes or until a toothpick inserted into the center comes out clean. Serve the cake plain or with an icing of confectioners' sugar.

Yogurt Cake with Cinnamon Syrup

Makes a 9-by-13-inch cake

Tickets to the Harvard-Yale football game are hot Cambridge commodities, and the fall frenzy of ticket-seekers can be fun to observe. Georgia Contos has the best view of the scramble from her desk in the ticket office of Harvard's athletic building.

"Our biggest chuckle is fans who come the day before the Yale game asking if there's something on the fifty yard line," she says. Then there's the father-in-law wanting seats at least thirty yards from his son-in-law, and the recently divorced woman whose "ex" has her ticket. Contos tries to solve all the problems while mailing schedules, answering phones, and selling tickets in the booth.

The one way to assure getting seats for big games is to buy season tickets, Contos advises, although she has never seen a Yale game herself — or a Dartmouth game, for that matter, or a Beanpot Hockey Tournament. The truth is that Contos, after twenty years at the University, has never set foot inside Harvard Stadium. "I work hard at the office. Then I draw the line and go home." There she thinks very little of sports while baking sweet cakes for her family of fans.

THE CAKE

    2 sticks butter
    2 cups sugar (½ L)
    5 eggs, beaten
    1 cup plain yogurt (¼ L)
    ½ teaspoon baking soda
    ½ cup milk (1 dL)
    3 cups sifted flour (¾ L)
    3 teaspoons baking powder

Before beginning, have the butter, eggs, yogurt, and milk at room temperature. Beat the butter until light and creamy. Add the sugar gradually and continue beating. Stir in the beaten eggs and yogurt. Combine the baking soda with the milk and blend into the mixture. Sift together the flour and baking powder. Add this gradually, beating until the batter is smooth.

Pour the batter into a greased 9-by-13-inch baking pan. Bake at 325°F (165°C) for 1 hour until the cake is light brown on top and springs back when lightly touched in the center. Cut the cake into serving pieces while it is still hot.

THE SYRUP

    1½ cups sugar (3½ dL)
    2½ cups water (6 dL)
    ¼–½ teaspoon cinnamon
    1 cup chopped walnuts (¼ L)

While the cake is baking, prepare the cinnamon syrup. In a saucepan, combine the sugar, water, and cinnamon.

Simmer 20–25 minutes, stirring frequently. Remove the saucepan from the heat and allow the syrup to cool. Pour the cooled syrup over the cake and promptly sprinkle the chopped nuts on top.

Labor-Intensive Pumpkin Chiffon Pie

Makes 2 9-inch pies

B etter known as an arbitrator than as a chef, former Secretary of Labor John T. Dunlop has functioned as both. Dunlop was a professor's cook during his undergraduate years in California. Today he is a professor himself — the Lamont University Professor at Harvard's Business School. After his classes on industry and government, Dunlop enjoys working in his own kitchen. This recipe of his calls for more effort than the standard pumpkin dessert, but then, the work yields *two* chiffon pies, and the delicate flavor is well worth the labor.

   3 eggs, separated
   1 cup sugar (¼ L)
   1 1-pound can pumpkin (46 dkg)
  ½ cup milk (1 dL)
  ½ teaspoon salt
  ½ teaspoon ginger
  ½ teaspoon cinnamon
  ½ teaspoon nutmeg
   1 tablespoon unflavored gelatin
  ¼ cup cold water (½ dL)
   2 9-inch single-crust pastry shells, baked

Combine the egg yolks and half the sugar and beat until thick. Pour the mixture into the top of a double boiler. Add the pumpkin, milk, salt, and spices, stirring to blend thoroughly. Cook in the double boiler, stirring frequently, until the mixture thickens. Remove the pot from the heat.

Soften the gelatin in the cold water, stirring until it dissolves. Beat the egg whites until they are thick. Add the remaining sugar and beat until the egg whites form soft peaks. Stir ⅓ of the beaten egg whites into the pumpkin mixture. Gently fold in the rest. Pour the mixture into the baked pastry shells and refrigerate them for several hours, until set. Serve plain or with whipped cream.

Walnut and Brandy Pie

Makes a 9-inch pie

Rachael Bornstein is a matchmaker. As a secretary for international programs at the Harvard Medical School, she introduces visiting physicians to Boston doctors in the same field. When cooking, Bornstein pairs taste with convenience. Try getting together with her rich American pie, which is easily made well in advance of a party.

4½ cups miniature marshmallows (11 dL)
6 tablespoons hot black coffee
1 pint heavy cream (½ L)
½ cup chopped walnuts (1 dL)
2 tablespoons brandy
1 9-inch graham-cracker-crumb pie shell, baked
shaved chocolate for garnish

Place the marshmallows in a saucepan. Add the hot coffee and cook over low heat, stirring constantly, until the marshmallows have dissolved and the mixture is completely smooth. Pour the mixture into a large bowl and let it cool to room temperature. Whip the cream until it forms soft peaks. Stir ⅓ of the cream into the marshmallow mixture. Gently fold in the rest. Fold in the walnuts and brandy. Pour the mixture into the prepared pie shell and refrigerate for several hours until firm enough to slice. Garnish with shaved chocolate.

Fudge-Bottom Pie

Makes a 9-inch pie

Radcliffe's Schlesinger Library houses some 20,000 volumes on the history of women in America, including a wealth of material on women's suffrage, trade unions, and cookery.

Barbara Haber is the curator of printed books at the library and is the author of a catalog of books on American women. Although she sometimes consults the stacks for a recipe, Haber has developed her own batch of favorites. Her vanilla pudding pie with a rich chocolate bottom actually comes from a Midwestern resource. Haber first encountered it in the student union at the University of Wisconsin, where it was made with country-fresh dairy products.

     1 6-ounce package chocolate chips (17 dkg)
    2¾ cups milk (7 dL)
     2 3-ounce packages vanilla pudding mix (170 g total)
     ½ pint heavy cream (¼ L)
     1 9-inch graham-cracker-crumb pie shell, baked

Reserve a small handful of the chips for the topping. Place the rest in a double boiler and melt over low heat, stirring occasionally. Add ¼ cup (½ dL) of the milk. Cook for 10 minutes, stirring occasionally, until thoroughly blended. Let the mixture cool to room temperature.

Pour the cooled chocolate into the pie shell. Using the back of a spoon, draw the chocolate up along the sides of the shell. Refrigerate the fudge-bottom pie shell while preparing the pudding.

In a saucepan, combine the vanilla pudding with the remaining milk. Cook over low heat, whisking constantly, until the mixture begins to boil. Remove the saucepan from the heat and place waxed paper on top of the pudding so that no skin forms. Let the pudding cool to room temperature.

Whip the cream until it forms soft peaks. Reserve ⅓ cup (¾ dL) for garnish. Stir half of the remaining whipped cream into the cooled pudding. Gently fold in the rest. Pour the mixture into the fudge-bottom pie shell. Spread the reserved whipped cream on top. Chop the reserved chocolate chips on a wooden board. Sprinkle the chocolate shreds on the whipped cream.

Hasty Pudding

Serves 8–10

The Harvard juniors who gathered around a boiling caldron of cornmeal-molasses mush in 1795 didn't know they would be remembered as founders of the world's third-oldest theatrical organization. For nearly

The sun had sunk; the melancholy knell
That lately moaned from the common's bell
Was hear'd no more; a deadly silence hung
O'er nature's works, and chained each gabbling tongue
When, lo, by every eye and mouth rever'd,
In Noyes' room the awful *pot* appear'd.

This verse and illustration are by Washington Allston, secretary of the Hasty Pudding Club in 1799. Washington's rhymes are in keeping with Pudding tradition, which requires that the minutes be recorded in verse. The history is preserved in the "Secretarys Records," a delicate diary kept in the Harvard University Archives.

a hundred years after that first meeting, the "Hasty Pudding" was strictly a social club for juniors who liked to smoke, drink, and engage in other activities that weren't allowed on Harvard property. Initiation rites were dramatic, incorporating masks, black sheets, and skulls. They culminated when the presiding officer thrust a spoonful of pudding at the initiate, commanding, "Brother, taste our coarse fare."

Debates, bawdy songs, and mock trials were popular

amusements at the Pudding until 1882, when the club produced its first operetta. Thus was established the annual tradition of witty drag-show musicals that still delight audiences at Harvard as well as road-show audiences in New York and Bermuda.

The pudding that was foisted on eighteenth-century initiates is documented below in a recipe taken from the club's files. It is now, as it was in 1795, coarse, lumpy fare.

½ gallon milk (2 L)
2 tablespoons butter
1 cup yellow cornmeal (¼ L)
1 quart cold milk (1 L)
1½ cups molasses (3½ dL)
1 cup sugar (¼ L)
1 tablespoon ginger
½ tablespoon salt

Place the half gallon of milk and the butter in a large pot or heavy casserole. Cook over high heat to scald the milk. Reduce the heat, add the cornmeal, and cook for 10 minutes, stirring constantly. Stir in the quart of cold milk and the molasses, sugar, ginger, and salt.

Bake in a long shallow dish at 350°F (180°C) for 1½ hours, stirring every 30 minutes. Let the pudding stand for several minutes before serving.

To spruce up hasty pudding, try a scoop of vanilla ice cream, a bit of maple syrup, or both.

Adam and Eve make themselves aprons of fig leaves in this woodcut from a sixteenth-century Bible. The black circles that appear on the left side of the arch (nearly on target for organic censorship), manifest the journey of a couple of book-worms. The Bible is housed at the Andover-Harvard Theological Library.

Glass Flowers Fig Pudding

Serves 12–14

The Glass Flowers are Harvard's main tourist attraction, drawing some 200,000 visitors each year. These botanical models depict 780 plant species, and they bloom all year at the Botanical Museum.

Leopold and Rudolph Blaschka — nineteenth-century artists and naturalists, father and son — created this hand-crafted, hand-painted garden in glass. Their models, certainly lovely to look at, are even more highly valued as instructional tools. Nowhere else can students, in a matter of hours, examine three-dimensional representatives of the entire plant kingdom in natural color and size.

Richard Schultes became interested in the Glass Flowers and botany during his years as a Harvard undergraduate. Now the Paul C. Mangelsdorf Professor of Natural Sciences, Schultes teaches botany at Harvard and serves as the director of the Botanical Museum. Sometimes he offers a Summer School course on plants of the Bible. Figs, he points out, are the first and most frequently cited fruit in the scriptures. They are also the key ingredient in his pudding, a cakelike creation in the plum pudding family.

    1 stick butter, softened
    2 eggs
    1 cup brown sugar or molasses (¼ L)
    2 cups finely chopped dried figs (½ L)
       grated rind of 1 lemon
    1 cup milk (¼ L)
  2½ cups sifted flour (6 dL)
    2 teaspoons baking powder
   ¾ teaspoon baking soda
    1 teaspoon salt
    1 teaspoon nutmeg, cinnamon, or ginger
   ½ teaspoon cloves

Beat the butter until it is light and fluffy. Add the eggs and brown sugar and beat thoroughly. Add the figs, lemon rind, and milk. Stir to mix well. Sift together the flour, baking powder, baking soda, salt, and spices. Gradually stir this into the fig mixture. Pour this batter into a greased 9-inch tube pan. Bake at 325°F (165°C) for 1 hour.

Schultes notes that the pudding may be eaten plain or with cream, lemon sauce, or hot red-wine sauce.

Baked Bananas with Rum

Serves 4

During World War II, botanist Richard Howard taught "survival dining" to Air Corps troops bound for the Pacific tropics. (A typical training meal featured avocado and alligator.) As a director of Harvard's Arnold Arboretum for twenty-five years, he later taught a course on botany in Boston restaurants.

Currently a professor of dendrology at Harvard, Howard teaches classes about trees and shrubs. His research is based in the Lesser Antilles, where bananas abound both in trees and desserts. Here's his Caribbean recipe for *Musa sapientum,* baked with spices, lime juice, and rum.

> 4 bananas, peeled and sliced lengthwise
> ½ teaspoon lime juice
> 1 tablespoon rum
> 1 tablespoon water
> 2 tablespoons sugar
>   nutmeg to taste
>   ground cloves to taste
>   allspice to taste
> ½ pint heavy cream (¼ L)

Place the bananas in a lightly greased baking dish. In a small bowl, combine the lime juice, rum, water, and sugar. Add spices and stir to blend thoroughly. Spoon the mixture over the bananas. Bake at 350°F (180°C) for 20 minutes.

Serve with cream or whipped cream. Chopped nuts and shaved chocolate also make good toppings, although the dessert is rich and delicious with cream alone.

To His Grace the
Duke of Chaulnes
President of the Royal Academy of Science
at PARIS &c..

G.D. Ehret. delin. & sculp.

From The Natural History of Barbados, *published in London in 1750, comes this illustration of* Musa sapientum. *The book by Griffeth Hughes, featuring art by G. D. Ehret, is among the resources in Harvard's Arnold Arboretum Library.*

Harvard history is dotted with student protests over food, like the riot this skeptic is about to incite. The illustration was a gift to the Harvard University Archives.

Curried Fruit Compote

Serves 6–8

Food — or the lack of it — has been known to make history. As a Marxist and assistant professor of history, Molly Nolan raises culinary issues (like the eighteenth-century transition from brown to white bread) while lecturing on Europe and the working class. Nolan's recipe for baked curried fruit may not make the history books, but it's definitely worthy of inclusion here.

(270)

7 cups sliced fruit*
⅓ cup butter (¾ dL)
⅔ cup brown sugar (1½ dL)
1 tablespoon curry powder
¼ teaspoon ground cloves
¼ teaspoon cinnamon

Place the fruit in a large baking dish. Melt the butter in a saucepan and add the brown sugar and spices. Cook over low heat, stirring constantly, until the sauce is smooth. Pour it over the fruit. Cover and bake at 350°F (180°C) for 1 hour. Serve topped with plain yogurt or vanilla ice cream.

Grapefruit Alaska

Serves 2

Cindy Witman offers a dessert that will grace any table. A 1977 graduate of the Harvard Divinity School, Witman is now a Methodist minister in a Minnesota parish. Her baked grapefruit à la mode with a meringue topping makes a simple refreshing dessert for two people.

1 grapefruit
2 egg whites
2 tablespoons sugar
2 scoops vanilla ice cream

Cut the grapefruit in half along its equator and scoop the pulp into a bowl. Discard the seeds and separate the pulp

* Fresh fruits work particularly well in this dish. Try pineapple, pears, apricots, peaches, bananas, apples, nectarines, cherries.

into bite-sized pieces. Beat the egg whites until they are foamy. Add the sugar and beat until they form soft peaks.

Arrange the hollow grapefruit halves in a baking dish and place a scoop of ice cream in each. Spoon the grapefruit pulp and a little juice on top. Spoon on the egg white meringue to completely cover the ice cream and grapefruit topping. Broil for about 20 seconds until the meringue turns light brown.

Rum Peaches with Cream

Serves 4

Chuck Coulson is clearly a man who loves eating. Large, twinkly-eyed, and glad to talk food, he has managed the Harvard Faculty Club for several decades. Coulson's desk is cluttered with culinary correspondence — plans for the overseers' dinners, the council-of-deans' lunches, and weekly Faculty Club fare. He can still locate, amid the chaos, the menu used during the visit of Queen Margrethe II of Denmark: crab-meat bisque, roast tenderloin of beef bordelaise, and fresh pineapple with kirsch and coconut.

Coulson, an alumnus of the Cornell Graduate School of Hotel Administration, lives with his family in a Faculty Club suite. In his public life he serves nearly two hundred guests daily. Privately, too, he's an enthusiastic host. Coulson favors these peaches as a dinner party dessert because they're so tasty and easy to make. The topping of brown sugar blended with sour cream, which makes such a fine year-round dish with canned peaches, works nicely with fresh fruits in season as well.

"Old Bailey Justice After Dinner," an English cartoon, is part
of the print collection at the Harvard Law School Library.

  1 20-ounce can of halved cling peaches in heavy syrup
     (57 dkg)
1–2 tablespoons light rum
  1 cup sour cream (¼ L)
 ¼ cup brown sugar (½ dL)
  1 cup toasted slivered almonds (¼ L)

Combine the peaches and their syrup with the rum in a
bowl. Cover and refrigerate overnight. Blend the sour
cream and brown sugar. Serve the peaches in fruit cups,
topped with the sour cream mixture and toasted almonds.

Fruit Kebabs Dipped in Cold Chocolate Fondue

Serves 8

For chocolate lovers who just can't get enough, a class called Chocolate Orgy may provide satisfaction. Ann Jones and Glen Allison are the masters of this kind of therapy, which they provide at the Cambridge Center for Adult Education.

Outside the chocolate group, Jones coordinates the community health and education projects sponsored by the Graduate School of Public Health. Allison, who spent two years at the Harvard Extension School and a summer in a Cambridge factory making peanut-butter kisses, is now a pre-med student at the University of Massachusetts.

The team's classroom menu runs from chicken to mousse, with chocolate a component of every dish. One of their lessons featured this dessert, with its thick chocolate sauce laced with coconut cream and Amaretto.

THE FONDUE

½ cup coconut cream or piña colada mix (1 dL)
½ pint heavy cream (¼ L)
½ cup condensed milk (1 dL)
1–2 tablespoons Amaretto
½ teaspoon vanilla extract
2–3 tablespoons Dutch cocoa

THE KEBABS

1 cup slivered almonds (¼ L)
1¼ cups shredded coconut (3 dL)

2 cups dried apricots, pitted figs, and dates (½ L)
2 cups fresh fruit*

To make the chocolatee fondue, whirl the ingredients in a blender until smooth. Pour the fondue into a bowl. Cover and freeze for 1 hour until the mixture thickens slightly.

To make the kebabs, grind the almonds in a hand-held rotary grater or process them in a blender until light and powdery. In a bowl, combine the ground almonds with the shredded coconut. Toss the dried and fresh fruits in the mixture to coat. Skewer the fruit (or have guests skewer their own).

When the fondue has been in the freezer for 1 hour, remove it and place it in a chafing dish over ice. Serve the fondue as a dip for kebabs.

Leftover fondue, laced with almond-coconut shreds, makes an excellent sauce for ice cream.

Muscovite of Strawberries

Serves 8

Barbara Wheaton's family got used to strange desserts after sampling Victorian ice creams for over five months. Wheaton, a culinary historian who studied art history at Radcliffe, updated dozens of nineteenth-century recipes for *Ices Plain and Fancy,* published by New York's Metropolitan Museum of Art.

Wheaton's husband and her youngest son were drafted as tasters, and they didn't hesitate to offer their critiques.

* Try pineapples, bananas, apples, pears, oranges, pitted cherries.

The garde-manger *or cold kitchen of nineteenth-century France was used for making ice creams, aspics, and the like. This illustration comes from Urbain Dubois's* Cuisine Artistique, *housed in Radcliffe's Schlesinger Library.*

Although cucumber ice won their reluctant approval and iced curried sole suffered a unanimous thumbs down, some desserts did earn genuine praise. Strawberries muscovite is one such success. Its flavor resembles that of a strawberry snow cone but its appearance is much more sophisticated: a frosty pink ring mold, garnished with whipped cream and sugar-dusted strawberries.

3 **cups ripe fresh strawberries (¾ L)**
½ **tablespoon powdered gelatin**
¼ **cup cold water (½ dL)**
¾ **cup sugar (1¾ dL)**
2¼ **cups hot water (5½ dL)**
    juice of 1 lemon

½ tablespoon crème de noyeau or other liqueur
whipped cream for topping

Purée 2 cups (½ L) of the strawberries in a blender or
food processor, or pass them through a food mill. Place
the gelatin in a bowl, add the cold water, and let stand
for 5 minutes. Add the sugar and hot water, stirring until
the gelatin and sugar are dissolved. Let the mixture cool.

Combine the puréed fruit with the gelatin mixture. Add
the lemon juice and liqueur. Pour into a mold and freeze
until solid, about 2–4 hours.

Just before serving, unmold onto a serving platter. Garnish with whipped cream (Wheaton uses a pastry bag
fitted with a star tube) and the remaining strawberries,
whole or sliced, dusted with sugar.

Lemon-Milk Sherbet

Serves 4–6

Louise Talley learned to cook out of sheer necessity
while studying business administration at Radcliffe in 1956. Talley lived in a student cooperative
where once a week, ready or not, she was obliged to cook
a hearty supper for fifteen roommates.

Since leaving Cambridge, Talley has studied with a
number of culinary superstars, including Dorothy Sims
(of Cuisinart) and Simone Beck (in James Beard's
kitchen). Watch for her recipes in *Gourmet* magazine,
where they sometimes appear. Meanwhile, here's Talley's
recipe for a refreshing sherbet. The sherbet would have
served her well back in 1956. It's so easy and so good after
a heavy meal.

1¼ cups sugar (3 dL)
grated rind of 1 lemon
⅓ cup lemon juice (¾ dL)
2 cups milk (½ L)

Refrigerate a mixing bowl and beaters. In a bowl, combine the sugar, lemon rind, and lemon juice. Add the milk and stir until the sugar is dissolved. Pour the mixture into an ice tray and freeze until firm, 1–3 hours. Scrape the mixture into the chilled bowl and beat with the chilled beaters until light and creamy. Return the mixture to the ice tray and freeze until firm. Talley serves her sherbet in chilled crystal bowls or champagne glasses and garnishes it with mint leaves.

Cinnamon Pastries with Lemon Glaze

Makes 16

Each winter Marie Marino supervises the Watson Skating Rink at Harvard. When the hockey team arrives she helps schedule practices. When the figure skaters glide in she takes charge of the record player. Spring finds Marino at the Weld Boat House, coordinating crew practices and checking students' identification. On Fridays, regardless of season or locale, Marino serves pastry to her athletic companions. These sugary snacks are now her trademark — at the rink, around the boat house, and in calmer environs.

THE PASTRIES

    2 3-ounce packages cream cheese, softened
       (170 g total)
    1 egg yolk, beaten
    ¼ cup sugar (½ dL)
    1 teaspoon cinnamon
    1 teaspoon lemon juice
    2 8-ounce packages prepared crescent rolls
       (45 dkg total)*

THE GLAZE

    1 cup confectioners' sugar (¼ L)
    2 tablespoons water
    1 teaspoon lemon juice
    ¼ cup finely chopped walnuts for garnish (½ dL)

In a small bowl, combine the cream cheese, egg yolk, sugar, cinnamon, and lemon juice. Stir to blend thoroughly. Place a teaspoon of this filling in the center of each dough triangle. Fold the top and one of the sides into the middle. Take the remaining corner and tuck it in so that no filling can escape. (If the resulting shape is that of a confused triangle, your pastries resemble those made by Marino.) Place the pastries on a lightly greased cookie sheet. Bake at 350°F (180°C) for 15 minutes. Remove the pastries and place them on cooling racks.

To make the glaze, combine the confectioners' sugar, water, and lemon juice. Place a sheet of waxed paper under the cooling racks. Drizzle the glaze over the still-warm pastries. Promptly sprinkle the chopped nuts on top. Let stand for several minutes before serving.

* Or make 16 puff-pastry triangles with a 2½-inch base.

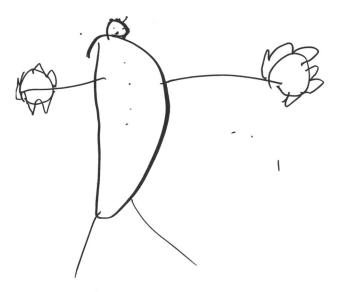

This preschooler has made so much "banana bread with nuts," he's starting to resemble a banana himself. Joshua Frazier, a preschooler at Harvard's Soldier's Field Park Children's Center, depicts a classmate in action during day-care cooking class.

Day Care Cookies

Makes 15–20

There are five day care centers and one nursery school at Harvard, scattered from Radcliffe to the far side of the Charles. Although the centers occupy Harvard property, they are incorporated independently and funded by tuition. The parents (students, faculty members, employees) do their part to keep tuition fees down by helping with teaching and cleaning up.

The "students," from two months to five years of age, can enjoy a Harvard education at the infant, toddler, or preschool level. The toddlers and preschoolers like this cooking exercise, with its rolling and patting, and its edible results. It makes an excellent project for a child between the ages of 1½ and 5, or for an adult in quest of the 8-minute cookie.

  1 cup Bisquick (¼ L)
  1 3-ounce package instant chocolate pudding (85 g)
  ¼ cup vegetable oil (½ dL)
  1 egg, lightly beaten

Combine all ingredients in a bowl and stir to blend thoroughly. Roll the mixture into balls and place them on a lightly greased cookie sheet. Press the balls flat with the palm of the hand. Bake at 350°F (180°C) for 8 minutes. Vary the recipe by using a different flavor of instant pudding or by decorating the surface of the cookies with chocolate chips or raisins.

Chocolate Covered Toffee Bars

Makes about 5 dozen

A t this point there is really no way to avoid it. Melanie Marcus (that's me — I'm the *Harvard Magazine* editor who compiled this collection) now faces the dilemma of all cookbook contributors: choosing a single recipe for posterity.

I first thought I'd go with something straightforward, like an appetizer of bacon and pickled watermelon rind on toothpicks. I like that combination, but it's ridiculously

This trade card once carried by a salesman for cocoa is now found at the Baker Library of Harvard's Graduate School of Business Administration.

simple. Besides, the hors d'oeuvre chapter seemed complete as it was.

Then I considered documenting a favorite spicy salad dressing, which announces each vegetable like a sharp bugle call. The mixture of lime juice and safflower oil with crushed ginger, garlic, and anise seed really perks up a salad, but perhaps other people like a bit less pizzazz. Eventually, while scrutinizing the chapter on desserts, I realized that it lacked a nice holiday cookie. My mother, as always, had just the thing. For as long as I can remember, her dainty toffee wafers have heralded the New Year at our home in Virginia.

2 sticks butter, softened
1 cup brown sugar (¼ L)
1 egg yolk
1 teaspoon vanilla extract
2 cups sifted flour (½ L)
1 6-ounce package chocolate chips (17 dkg) *
1 cup walnuts, finely chopped

Cream the butter and sugar. Beat in the egg yolk and vanilla extract. Gradually add the flour, stirring to blend thoroughly. Spread the batter ¼ inch thick in a lightly greased 10-by-15-inch jelly roll pan. Bake at 350°F (180°C) for 20 minutes or until golden brown.

Remove the pan from the oven and turn off the heat. Sprinkle the chocolate chips over the surface. Replace the pan in the warm oven for 2–3 minutes. Remove the pan. Using a frosting spatula, spread the chocolate to cover the entire surface. Promptly sprinkle the chopped nuts on top. While warm, cut into 1-inch squares.

* This provides enough chocolate to lightly coat all the bars. True chocolate lovers will probably prefer to purchase a 12-ounce package (approximately 34 dkg of chocolate chips) and use about ¾ of the package.

Indices

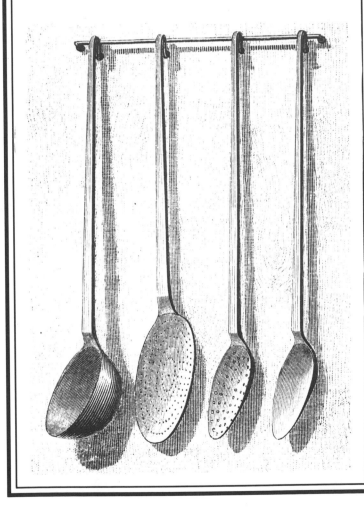

Index of Recipes

(287)

(290)

Index of People, Places, and Institutions

Radcliffe College, 49
Radcliffe Institute for Independent Study, 231
Radcliffe Quadrangle, 223, 246
Raven, Rachael, 62
Reed, Kit, xiv
Robert, Ann and Lucien, 157
Roberts, Rick, ix
Ronis, Lisa, 251
Rosen, George, 73
Rosen, Joel, 216
Rosen, Richard, 41
Rothman, Bill, 54
Russian Research Center, 11

Sassower, Carey, 85
Schlesinger Library, viii, 2, 3, 8, 13, 30, 36, 42, 46, 49, 58, 63, 78, 94, 102, 104, 107, 134, 176, 177, 184, 212, 228, 236, 250, 254, 262, 276, 286
Schmitt, Jack (Harrison), 201
Schrecker, Ellen, 231
Schroeder, Pat, 79
Schultes, Richard, 266–67
Science Center Library, 202
Sellmer, Richard, viii
Semitic Museum, viii, 237
Shapiro, Jim, ix. 7, 152
Shapiro, Laura, 26–27
Shaw, Diana, viii, 53
Shioji, Hiroki, 147
Signet Society, 161
Silverman, Fran, 46
Singer, Martha, 164
Skinner, B. F., 145
Smith, Cynthia, 103
Smith, Fred, 103
Soldiers' Field Park Children's Center, 280–81

Southern, Eileen, 137
Steadman, Richard, 66
Stevenson, Adlai III, 128
Sullivan, Ed, 180

Tait, Kate, 161
Talley, Louise, 277
Tennermann, Bill, ix
Teeter, Anita, 197
Teeter, Karl V., 197
Tolentino, Tony, 217
Toomre, Joyce, 12–13
Torrey, Jennifer, viii
Trager, James, 243
Tryon, Alice, 118
Tyron, Rolla, 118

Villa I Tatti, 198
Vosgerchian, Luise, 6

Wald, George, 105
Warren, Maurie, 227
Watkins, Jane, 24
Watson Skating Rink, 278
Weld Boat House, 278
Weinstock, Gerry, 9
Weissbecker, Frank, 125–26
Wheaton, Barbara, viii, 3, 275
Widener Library, 83
William James Hall, 145, 223
Wilson, Edwin O., xv, 119
Witman, Cindy, 271
Wornson, Doug, 142
Wyatt, Faye, 169
Wyatt, Joe, 169
Wylie, Laurence, 171

Young, Burris, 39

(300)